the mexican stove

Sensual and Evocative Notes

on the World's Oldest Cuisine

Together with Matchless

Methods for Cooking and Eating

Such Timelessness

and including

The Oldest Surviving, Evolved

Recipe for Cooked Food

of any Cooking System of any

of the Ancient Civilizations

of the World and the

Greatest All-purpose Sauce

in History

RICHARD CONDON / WENDY BENNETT

the mexican stove

WHAT TO PUT ON IT AND IN IT

DOUBLEDAY & COMPANY, INC., GARDEN CITY, NEW YORK

Books by Richard Condon

AND THEN WE MOVED TO ROSSENARA

ARIGATO

THE VERTICAL SMILE

MILE HIGH

THE ECSTASY BUSINESS

ANY GOD WILL DO

AN INFINITY OF MIRRORS

A TALENT FOR LOVING

SOME ANGRY ANGEL

THE MANCHURIAN CANDIDATE

THE OLDEST CONFESSION

Designed by Joseph P. Ascherl

ISBN: 0-385-03427-x
Library of Congress Catalog Card Number 72–89299

For
Judith van Beuren
Anita Brenner
Rosa Covarrubias
and
Carmen López-Figueroa
who know all the secrets

Now let me say farewell, great God, little mama!
While I slice an apple, heaven of my heart;
I came to entertain you, great God, little mama!
Now so long until tomorrow, heaven of my heart.

Zandunga, song of Tehuantepec

CONTENTS

traditions of mexican cuisine

he dominant number of Mexicans are healthy, humorous, and numerous. The many-splendored food they eat evolved those three attractive qualities. When J. A. Brillat-Savarin, a name which, belonging in every food book, should be disposed of at the earliest, wrote: "Tell me what you eat and I'll tell you what you are," the mandatory quotation for all food writers, he meant the inner you, not the national you. After all, the national dishes of the United States are spaghetti, hamburgers, and hot dogs (eaten at separate meals, thank Victua, Goddess of Gastronomy). If you told the man that was what you ate he wouldn't tab you as being Italian or German but as being peer-groupish, unimaginative, or even lazy.

All food appeals to some senses, only great food to all senses; but then to an elevated degree. Canned salmon and All-Bran do not have great sight appeal, except for the packages, but they do appeal to the sense of touch. The pop which follows the bite into a kosher frankfurter even allows the sense of hearing to participate in the American process of being rid of having to eat; that tiresome prelude to heartburn and burping.

However, in the instance of the most exalted food ever to appear in the Western Hemisphere, the food whose raw materials became the parents of all European cooking, it becomes evident, when the glorious plunge is taken, that to cook and eat Mexican food is to celebrate sensuality in every great chamber of this textured, perfumed, delicious, beautiful, and memorable gastronomic antiquity.

Mexican food is an aphrodisiac which excites the passion for living. It courts, seduces, ravishes, then cherishes all five senses (as well as the sense of most worthy accomplishment) by treating each as if it existed alone, as if all satisfaction were dependent upon this one sense, while it orchestrates all five into complex permutations of sensation.

Almost three quarters of the way through this century and rushing forward like a sealed train, we find ourselves inhabiting what can only be called an interregnum of the senses. That is, we hope keenly that we are between two rules of sensing, that proper sensing has not just stopped altogether as another victim of modern distribution. We know that large units of the Western population are trying to establish that it is time to supplant the sensual benefits of alcohol with blander elements of the pharmacy. Music is a paralyzed form. The novel has married pornography, which oddly lacks sensation; painting is mainly witless and trendy. The leaders of the war by women against men have gone well beyond implying that the sudden discovery of the clitoris makes men unnecessary and have begun to insist on this with odd leers. Tobacco is being phased out along with previous sensualities of religious ecstasy. The intense masochistic pleasure of wars has been boldly appropriated for the enjoyment of an elite of black youths and socially recalcitrant white boys (and their parents), and the well-to-do need not apply. Fashion, which once changed with the calendar from the center of the sun in Paris, is gone without memory of loss and well beyond the memory of the senses. Tension has become more desirable than serenity.

The most barren desert of this interregnum is the food we are allowed to eat. Status chewing is dictated mainly by the purse, but money can take one only so far. What with the smoking during meals and the bourbon and water beside the plate representing the wine of the country, most people are doing pretty well if they can tell cornflakes from clams.

Western food excites the sense of sight, to be sure, then it stops right there. Mexico is indeed in the West but its food has been Eastern in concept and development for at least six thousand years. With North American food, the brilliant, cosmetic appearance of the food itself, loaded with dyes, preservatives, chemicals, and roughage, sets off the gastric juices, satisfies nothing in an ancient memory which

says vaguely that food should also taste (at least), then sends the feeder away refueled but made one mealtime more barbaric. The Elberta peach is exquisitely flavorsome but is bypassed because its pale flesh makes it less attractive than the California cling peach, which has little flavor at all. It took the businessmen a lot of time to persuade the market that distribution must come before a silly pleasure such as eating and that it is axiomatic that whatever looks delicious tastes and smells delicious; future anthropologists will fix on Coca-Cola as being the vintage wine of our day.

It is not as hard on the market as it sounds. Our wonderful overcommunications industry, led by a television technology and merchandising force which is unsurpassed, has, in one generation, the mere twenty-five years since 1947 when Uncle Milty first wore a lady's hat on the friendly, tiny screen, habituated the West into becoming a culture of voyeurs whose salivation starts and stops with and at the sensations imagined by sight.

So we eat the straw with thiamin added which has been scientifically blended with soupçons of blotting paper and a dash of sawdust and call it bread. We are confused into imagining that it should also taste, smell, and resound with the delighted squeals of every chewer while its glossal and tacto-dental textures combine in glorious contrast on many levels of gastronomic design. We need not regret really because there are cookery books to remember those things for us and to tell us how it used to be; printed memory cores which serve as surrogate for the conditioned sense we have come to depend upon best—the sense of sight, the genitalia of the voyeur—while not requiring us to gain one ounce.

Most people want it that way. Food is for snobs and takes too much time to eat. The entire world, which is to say the nations of five continents, eagerly shares this food: canned baked beans, canned salmon, frozen chickens, fish fingers, frozen peas, white flour, canned pineapple, granulated sugar, Coca-Cola, and scotch whiskey. No matter how remote from the Western mainstream, the tribes become addicted to Western food. Dr. Magnus Pyke, the leading Scottish nutritionist, says it has become more and more difficult to study Australian aborigines and Eskimos eating their traditional food. This food-sampling process begins with the increment of Hilton hotels, or their equivalent, which brings this sterile gookum to all the nations of the earth.

That Mexican food is still recognizable as existing for delectation today as it existed six thousand years ago is a result not of gastronomic mirror worship but of the fact that their food is so infinitely superior in the courtship of the senses over "well-distributed food" that Mexicans, to a most gallant extent which, alas, is not total, resist the temptations of canned ravioli and tinned chocolate pudding.

Mexicans have television but they fight off TV dinners at a time when the people living in the Colossus of the North don't have the strength at the end of the day to do much more than to slide a TV dinner into an oven in all the balanced colors and a fit sense of presentation of what beautiful food should look like. That there used to be people, non-pros, who could hang in a kitchen for hours and hours just to turn out one meal is a conception which is becoming part of American folklore. "Beefsteaks" are being manufactured in Minneapolis, made out of spun soybeans, and when your turn comes around to try these you can bet they will be sensational-looking steaks, maybe two inches thick, at the price of a plastic pizza, served up with a charcoal crust and then—wow, Mom!—when the butter knife cuts through that tenderized goodness there will be a lovely pinkness bleeding there and sending up a cloud of steam. Man, I mean, like, what else, except that they will be copyright as Soyrloyn Stayks and the crew of forty-six are working on the TV commercials right now.

That's still a day away, maybe a half day away. Lot's wife knew what she was missing when she turned back to take a last look, so why can't we turn back to Mexican food before it is too late, to turn backward somewhere between four and six thousand years as though to prove that practice makes perfect?

Memory is the greatest factor in the enjoyment of food. Food memories are where all food prejudices are stored. I will not eat any of the fruits of the sea even though I know cooks can perform miracles with the stuff. Something in my memory, undoubtedly the still-remembered stench of the ill-kept fish shop of my childhood, tells me I do not like fish. Food traditions are group prejudices which allow people to admire the man who first swallowed an oyster. But the development of a system of food traditions which may be characterized as a "cuisine" takes considerable time. Saillant-Curnonsky, that other name required to appear in all food books, said: "One does not invent a new dish by pouring fish soup over a sirloin."

National feeding whims seem boundless. Europeans and Americans savor turtle but would reject iguana. Europeans prize the roe of the Persian sturgeon but would be appalled at being asked to eat the roe of an aquatic beetle as in Mexico, or brandied snakes' eggs as in Singapore. In Wonersh, Surrey, eating dogs is taboo, but the Mexican xoloizcuintle, that stubby, naked, perspiring, plump Colima dog, is bred to be eaten and, on market day in Tabasco, tethered at the butcher's, does its best to chew on the customers before the customers can chew on it. The Balinese enjoy eating fried baby bats; Chinese favor pink baby mice. Europeans roast six-week-old lambs. Americans can down gigantic West Coast oysters and, in Mexico, one delicacy is a sandwich made with live honey ants which then roam like champagne bubbles through the sinuses.

Magnus Pyke says: ". . . as the centuries have passed and human life has become more complex, the number of different edible foods which are actually eaten has dwindled." Distribution problems may account for that, and stockholders' reports, but the termites which are being eaten in the Congo, in an analysis of 561 calories per hundred grams, show 36 percent of protein and 44 percent of fat, which is superior to the yield of most other foods.

Mexican food-preparation systems are Asiatic. Just as the most comprehensive and artful of all cooking systems, the Chinese, evolved from Indian cuisine, it is said that Mexican cooking evolved from both of these while combining with the delicate and fetching Japanese. I disagree with that theory but only in the manner in which food historians say the trajectories of Mexican cuisine evolved.

Like Mom's apple pie, it took time. Cooks had to pull up roots at the Garden of Eden, somewhere in Afghanistan, to move east and be allowed to die after they had trained other, improved, cooks who moved east and farther east until they faced water, then started walking north toward the Bering Strait. It took ten or twelve thousand years and no one was rushing. While all those millennia of cooks were cooking, His eye was on the swallow.

I think perhaps they walked to Mexico and perhaps they floated. There are still great, almost mystically endowed native, uneducated navigators in the Pacific. But Eskimos, Amerinds, and Mexicans had to come from Asia. Put any fifty Mexicans into Japanese army fatigues and mix them with any fifty Japanese in the same sort of suits and it will be very difficult to tell them apart.

Mexican food is oriental in its traditions and in its race memory. Not only is it sensually triumphant but it has a wealth of health and more bounce to the ounce. Nutritional studies of the Otomí Indians in the Mezquital Valley of central Mexico who thrived in Mexico before the arrival of the Toltec or Aztec cultures, provide a long-term demonstration for Mexican food. In the present time, although their health is excellent, they eat few of the foods which are accepted in the Western society as being necessary to provide a nutritious diet. They eat little meat or dairy products or fruit or vegetables of conventional kinds. They eat tortillas and local plants such as malva, tuna, nopalea, maguey, yucca, sorrel, wild mustard flowers, and cactus fruit. They drink pulque, a light beer made from the century plant. When the components of the Otomí diet were analyzed at M.I.T., it was found that they provided better nutritional balance than was in the diet of a group of United States town dwellers who were surveyed simultaneously. Beyond the Otomí, the rural populations all over Mexico live on tortillas, corn, and beans —a most efficient balanced diet.

They also get to eat, now and again, from tables covered closely and pungently with such heavenly things as *quesadillas potosinas*, golden cheese decanted as in Potosí into capsules with the lightest crust; *chalupas estilo Puebla*, tissue-thin tortillas spread over with a green sauce; chiles in walnut sauce; enormous bowls of *mole negro oaxaqueño*, its texture and color of boiling chocolate throwing off a cinnamon steam and under which float tender chunks of turkey, peanuts, spareribs, pecans, raisins, and almonds; fire buckets of *salsa picante* and *pozole;* stacked quires of warm tortillas; hot maroon *frijoles rancheros* and enough *mochomos*, captured within a ring of green guacamole, which is the very color of springtime, to satisfy the hunger of a war party of Lipans. The smells of this food alone could nourish a sedentary worker; an ecumenicity of smells, textures, and flavors, each willing to welcome the other infidels into its congregation if it were immediately accepted as the flavor of flavors, the smell of smells, the sensation of all senses.

Mexican food is original in more ways than the design of its presentations and the systems of its preparation. It astounds one to learn that not one of the vegetables which were native to Mexico was known to Europe before the Conquest. These Mexican vegetables which somewhat enriched the fare of

Europe were tomatoes, corn, chocolate; lima beans, string beans, and shell beans; peanuts, Jerusalem artichokes, pumpkins, and squashes; pineapples, strawberries, blackberries, raspberries, and blueberries; guava, avocado, chestnuts, and pecans. Also, from other parts of the New World, came the first potatoes and coconuts. The potatoes, from Peru, came in many sizes and nine colors.

Of all the food imported from the New World the potato had the longest uphill climb to its eventual popularity. It was the first edible plant to be grown from tubers, not from seed. The damned stuff grew backward, forcing flesh-colored lumps underground. It had fingerlike growths which looked like the deformed hands and the bleached skin of leprosy so, throughout all Europe, the potato was believed to cause leprosy. Magnus Pyke says that if the New World had not yielded the potato until now, as an unknown food it would be banned by Pure Food and Drug authorities because potatoes contain a poisonous substance: solanine.

No one is more extraneous than a music or art critic unless it is someone who writes about food. It so often appears to be a pantomime of snobbism or eclecticism and, so very frequently, boobism. Not one of the three could persuade me that *Manon Lescaut*, Chagall, or fish was acceptable. But the fact is that chewing gum was also discovered in Mexico so Americans owe, at the very least, the debt of attention to that nation's other chewing accomplishments even though you might (presently) feel that it's all just a lot of nonsense about stuff which becomes fuel the instant it is swallowed because we are made of carbon and must burn the basic proteins, fats, and carbohydrates to keep going, so that part of it may be transformed into energy and the rest into chemicals, lubricants, and stimulants until, at last, from eating so much of it we finally die from it because the damned stuff burning like that has worn the machinery out. And you would be quite right. Nonetheless, the better the food the longer we may last, or at least the joy of eating it may make it seem to have lasted longer. In terms of fuel into energy, chemicals, lubricants, and stimulants, Mexican food is incomparable because it is lighter, more natural, less fatty, and at least 11° warmer inside. Furthermore, as a producer of joy and well-being only Chinese cuisine can surpass it and only the French can equal it.

2

Our credentials: (a) I am a former glutton whose appetites time has faded but who still chews wistfully on; (b) we lived in Mexico for a combined total of four years—i.e., I lived there for two years with the entire family, then Wendy married and returned to Mexico after, intermittently, having attended Mexico City College, where she took to cooking Mexican meals and to breeding a son named Benito-Juárez Bennett, who carries a Mexican passport; (c) to our supreme advantage, we had not tasted any Mexican food until we moved to Mexico City.

We moved to Mexico for two reasons. The first was that I wanted to write a novel called *A Talent for Loving*, which was to have a Mexican background in the years between 1844–71. Secondly, a friend of ours of sweet memory, Benn Reyes, had an idea that he could persuade all powers to allow him to stage a World's Fair in Mexico for which I was to become an "adviser." Reyes, who was a Mexican-American, and I arrived at that plateau of a city, nestled in a *valley* which is seventy-two hundred feet in the air and, as every good lowlander should, I got dizzy first, then sleepy, then with all the help of good friends reached the point of routine nausea which accompanies *altitudismo* for the first three days in record time. That is, if one walks slowly, rests frequently, and does not eat heavily or drink alcohol for three days, one will not feel the effects of the altitude at all.

However, Reyes' World's Fair Committee was waiting that first evening. We were taken on a walking tour of the rosé section of the city—where tourists look at the (Mexican) world through rose-colored glasses, seeing no poverty, no pain, no problems—and then entered a private dining room of La Fonda del Refugio, a heaven away from heaven for Mexican feeders, and only for me—just to give whey-faced, tottering North American me an *idea* of what the greatest Mexican food could be—the Committee kept it coming while Reyes pleaded grimly, sotto voce, to keep eating and not to risk offending these patriotic, key men by turning anything away. I should have slept in a casket that night just to show how efficient a patriotic, key American could be. The banquet ended with a chile-eating contest among the natives, who called for and ate hot, hotter, hottest chiles until only one man could whisper, so he won.

The next day, supported on the right by Reyes and on the left by our associate, Enrique López, I was somehow moved, upright, to a car which was to drive us to the home of the chairman of this whole misbegotten idea. I had been vigorously ill all night and had cheeks which could have been an advertisement for Dutch Boy white lead paint, so Reyes suggested that we stop and have "a little *barbacoa*" so that when we reached the chairman's and he offered us the scotch whiskey which was the inescapable status symbol in Mexico because it was so expensive, I would not faint. I did not know what *barbacoa* was. They took me to a lovely open park with tables like a Viennese beer garden except that this turned out to be a Mexican roast lamb garden.

The lamb of *barbacoa mexicana* is cooked in a pit in the ground which has been lined with *pencas,* the leaves of the maguey plant from which pulque is made. It's odd about pulque. Mexicans so believe in its power that a country fellow can get smashed on two bottles of it which would have the effect of two Cokes and an aspirin on any foreigner. Swedes have the same flawed faith in schnaps.

The *barbacoa* was so great that I ate six large hunks of this barbecued lamb wrapped in six large, warm tortillas. I felt marvelous. The dizziness and the nausea had gone away. I could walk with the stride of an eighty-year-old man to the car. We drove to the chairman's. The chairman served scotch whiskey and Reyes and López greatly admired the brand. Then the señora announced that dinner was served.

DINNER?

Never before in forty-four short years in forty-one countries, having lived for two years or more in five of those countries and having been a glutton by natural inclination, have I seen a dinner to equal the size and variety of that dinner and, twelve years later, I have never seen—no Jewish or Italian mother meal, no combinations of the food served in the Bernese Oberland and the Graubunden, where

dumplings are fired as large as basketballs in four-meats-and-twelve-vegetable stews—any array and weight and expanse of food to equal it. This woman and two cooks had to have been cooking for two days (by North American standards). Much later, when I came to understand the labors which must go into Mexican food preparation, I looked back and calculated that she must have started to cook six days before, twenty minutes after her husband had gotten the confirmation of the date we would leave New York.

Even López, born in Mexico and therefore adjusted to the altitude, which provided 11 percent less oxygen than at sea level, went pale as he stared at those tables. All Reyes was thinking of was the deal, and he remained as jaunty as if we faced a shallow dish of watercress sandwiches. All I was thinking of was survival. Reyes said to me, "A man's wife's cooking is a sacred rite here, please! Eat! Eat everything she puts down, please!"

Did that lady ever put down plates of food! There was a canoe filled with guacamole because the señora knew Americans liked guacamole. Then we all had some *sopa de flores de calabaza,* which is squash-blossom soup. It was wonderful soup. I wanted to weep because I had not trained for this meal. I wanted to kill these two twitty Mexicans, my partners, who had not told me what was going to happen to me in the chairman's house that afternoon and who had taken me to eat those goddamn *tacos de barbacoa*. Then—why not?—a little green rice to firm up the soup down dere dorten. Two little women staggered in from another room carrying a gigantic bowl of something which was jetting hot perfume. The señora hoped I enjoyed *mancha manteles*. Reyes explained that this was the second Mexican meal of my life, really the first, because it was the first Mexican meal I had ever eaten in a Mexican home, but that he knew that I would *love mancha manteles*. The señora beamed and instructed me to eat heartily, remembering that the translation of *mancha manteles* was: tablecloth stainer. I was sweating hard as she overdid me the honor of preparing my plate, a very wide plate, perhaps a foot in diameter. The tablecloth stainer contains the following: one turkey, four *chorizo* sausages, sliced pineapples, sliced apples, sliced bananas, some pork; *ancho*, *pasilla* and *serrano* chiles; almonds, cinnamon, lard, and tomato puree. Reyes scooped away as though he had picked up a fake stomach at Macy's. I got through it. I don't know how I did it. I felt like a passenger in a jet at thirty-two thousand feet after the cabin has sprung a leak and the oxygen masks won't drop. The dizziness and nausea were back, then something terrible happened. It was a day of famous firsts. The nice cool glass of drinking water I had had that morning and had repeated every time I felt

faint was preparing to deliver the dread blow of "Moctezuma's revenge." The señora was in the kitchen supervising the loading of the vehicles which would bring the next course to the table. I mumbled something urgent to López, who is a sympathetic man. He said something in rapid Spanish to the chairman. Both men, very experienced with gringos, leaped to their feet and, holding me by either arm, steered me to the loo. I was there for some time.

When I emerged the señora was ready with the *albóndigas*, which are Mexican meatballs, and a little speech about Mexican *albóndigas* telling why they were different from any other meatballs in the world because of what they contained. What they contained was: veal, pork, lamb, and ham; onions, bread, four eggs, and lard; a pound of green tomatoes, some vinegar, some *chipotle* chiles, coriander, parsley, and a quart of good, solid soup stock. Furthermore, the señora did me the honor of serving me directly, actually operating the loading crane which put the food on my newer, larger plate.

Much later, after the doctor left the hotel, Reyes told me that it was a very lucky thing that I happened to get Moctezuma's revenge just at those five times because while I was away from the table the señora had insisted that they all have seconds of everything. A very peculiar physiological metamorphosis happened to Reyes that afternoon. When he entered the chairman's house he was a well-set-up, definitely not stout fellow who spoke American with a marked California accent. After that dinner he was not only a stout man—and I mean a shorter, rounder, fatter man with a pronounced paunch—but his speech changed. He would ramble in the diction of a Negro jazz musician or break into voluble Spanish. Not that the señora's meal taught him to speak Spanish. He had always spoken Spanish. But never to Jewish delicatessen waiters, for example, or to austere British bootmakers.

We ate sweet bell peppers stuffed with beans, cream, cheese, tomatoes, oil, and oregano. We had Oaxaca tamales (which contain corn, lime, lard, turkey broth, banana leaves, spareribs, *chilhuacle* chiles and *mulato* chiles, almonds, walnuts, peanuts, tortillas, sesame, raisins, chocolate, bread, tomatoes, cloves, cinnamon, peppercorns, and oregano). We had ranch-style black beans from Morelos. Reyes swears that I was staying away from the table so long that I missed the stewed turtle from the señora's home state of Vera Cruz and the chiles in walnut sauce from Puebla which contained (he was sitting heavily in a chair in front of my bed at the hotel as he tried to tell me this and his diction had already begun to change): twelve bell peppers, four eggs, flour, lard, tomato puree, onions, garlic, ground pork, cinnamon, citrons, raisins, blanched almonds, four peaches, two pears, fifty shelled walnuts, goat's cheese, milk, a pomegranate, and chopped parsley.

He could not remember the desserts but he knew there had been more than one. López could not remember the desserts. I could not remember anything after the *mancha manteles*. Tablecloth stainer, indeed!

Reyes always held that my unaccountable fastidiousness had blown the World's Fair deal but there were many other reasons and we both knew that. The repast at the chairman's house was always referred to as "that typically Mexican meal."

I dragged you through all that to make this point: *despite* the most agonizing afternoon and evening of my life, *despite* the altitude illness and Moctezuma's revenge, *despite* how it changed Reyes' appearance and speech, I have to say that all of my senses fell wildly in love with Mexican food that afternoon until it has become one of the major passions of my life.

3

Despite the 361,593 separate editions currently in print which relate about the food of Europe (which derives from Mexican food products, if not methods), there have been relatively few books written about Mexican food and its preparation. However, the subject is so moving that most of these books are labors of love and, because they combine so much affection with scholarly curiosity, most are first-class books.

Mexican cuisine is something like a historical novel which has a gorgeously wanton redhead on its dust jacket. Perhaps within the novel, but most certainly within the presence of Mexican food, history, grandeur, violence, *amor*, and tyranny are offered to the jaded. Ten to twelve thousand years of chewing and tasting, of hiring and firing cooks, of arguing with butchers, are involved and—who knows?—ten or twelve thousand scents and flavors may have been lost in the undergrowths of those millennia.

American (and all but the most *haute* European) food exists by itself on one monotonous plateau—any Western meal being the equivalent, in music, to the *cantus firmus* of liturgical chanting or, in painting, to the rebus. Contrariwise, each dish prepared under Mexican food systems is multileveled and richly dimensional. It is thermally rich. It is scented. Its grasp of glossal tactility is uncanny and exciting as it composes dishes of food to relate the textures of the rough, the slippery, the chewy, and the unctuous simultaneously while it contrasts the hot, the bland, and the piquant with sweet, sour, and salt tastes and as it relates the readily combined flavors of meat, fruit, and vegetables with an astonishing range of sauces.

However, because it is high cooking, it takes a considerable amount of time to prepare. In the words of the sorcerers, spirits, and familiars of Señora Judith van Beuren, the most indefectible authority within or without Mexico on the food of Mexico, as artist-in-chief at La Fonda del Refugio in Calle Liverpool, Mexico City: "It is conceivable that a great Swiss, Italian, or Parisian chef can pick up a good Mexican cookbook (which must be one of the old ones) and, having instructed a pilot friend to fly him over some *mulato, pasilla, ancho, guajillo, cascabel, chile de árbol,* and *piquín,* plus *epazote, yerba santa,* sour oranges, a *nopal* with fruit, *aguacates, tomates de cáscara, plátanos machos,* fresh *serrano,* vanilla pods, cacao beans, and a *metate;* and, having established serene gladness and no visitors in his kitchen, produce a platter of fine *uchepos,* a good *mancha manteles* and a bowl of chilled *tunas* to finish off with. He can then go on to *romeritos* or a *mole* with *bayos de olla,* bake *charal* tamales and serve them with guacamole, *salsa casera,* and *frutas en vinagre,* tossing off some *quesadillas de flor* to go with the cocktails, a pitcher of *chía* to go with the food, and pass around a salver of crystallized *calabaza, camotes, biznaga,* and *chilacayote* with the *cafe de olla* at the end.

"It is conceivable, and this virtuoso would certainly rate and probably receive the Order of the Aztec Eagle from the nearest dazzled, homesick Mexican ambassador, as well as a visit from Maximilian's ghost, which shouldn't trouble such a one at all. Excepting him, it is just not possible to cook Mexican food that way. It is not necessarily the case that somebody's *nana* has to supervise the kitchen from which good Mexican food is expected to emerge, but it helps.

"However, you don't have to use a *metate* and it is possible, for example, to substitute freshly ground *masa* for tamales with the dehydrated kind, if you can find a good kind in your town. But to learn how to establish the progression of blends, or juxtapositions, to know *el punto*, and when to use *pasilla* and when you absolutely don't, there is no package. You have to find places where they make Mexican food without cheating on either time or quality; then, knowing how it is supposed to taste, look, and be served, you must practice it like Zen instructed by a master, in this case usually the old lady who knows how to fold herself with grace at the *metate*. But if there is no *nana* at hand, work at it via any good Mexican cook you know. You will acquire Zen virtues of surrender and humility, whereupon you will suddenly find yourself able to solo with many of the simpler things (or the most approachable in terms of ingredients) from good recipes. That is, if you have absorbed the feel of the thing, the style, the approach, and are yourself prepared to leap into change, variation, and discovery as every artist must. That is, perhaps, the really arcane secret of them all."

That was an outcry from one of the supreme artists of Mexican food. If you and I took Señora Van Beuren's perfectionism to heart we would cheat ourselves out of considerable gastronomic ecstasy because we would either have to save up, find the time and a sitter, and fly to Mexico to feed upon the penetrating sensuality of that food. Or we could take a step backward and seek out a Mexican or a "Mexican" restaurant nearer to where we live; but beyond California, the Southwest, and the big cities of the United States not enough of either one or the other seems to exist. The only way to control the glory—and then on the basis that practice makes perfect—is to cook one or two, then four or six, then eight or fourteen Mexican dishes in one's own kitchen. If time can be ignored, if patience and all the self-confidence of Prince Charles when he was young are available to you—all of it is far easier than one might think.

Wendy and I plunged into this book in Ireland, where, for four months in the summer of 1971 at Rossenarra, our little thatch on the *altiplano* of County Kilkenny, in the gourmet capital, Kilmoganny, Wendy test-cooked and recooked about ninety-seven Mexican dishes, across the courses from Aceituna to Zarzamora, from *sopas* to *postres*. Ireland isn't exactly a Zapotec's home away from home. In fact, we have written the first Mexican cookbook ever written in Ireland, even though writing has been practiced on just about everything else here from just after the glacier had receded and through the Viking occupation right up to the *Dublin Magazine*. In fact, we are told that it was the early Irish who founded the Northumberland school, at which the English were taught to read—which they now do very, very well.

The strategic problem of test-cooking Mexican recipes in Ireland, it might be thought, would be the characteristically Mexican supplies. Although the Irish are *muy charro* they do not eat with a daring palate. We made advance plans to work it all out with the Mexican consul in Dublin, a Mixteco named Don McGreevy, but that never became necessary. We were able to assemble a mighty larder, mainly from the dazzling array of foreign-food shops in Soho, London; from New York; and from Dublin's Smyth's-on-the-Green and the elegant food shops in Chatham Street. It was only necessary to have four dried chile varieties sent by air from friends in Mexico City. We lacked for nothing. Most particularly we did not lack for Guest Tasters, who ranged from such cunning cooks as Len Deighton to such crafty chewers as Mick Jagger, Elizabeth O'Driscoll, Desmond Guinness; John Bryson and Ferdinand Fairfax, photographers and eaters; James Richard Blake, portrait painter and taco consumer, Dr. David Hanly, a Gaelicist, and Mr. Anthony Godwin, a publisher of heavy books.

Wendy cooked for as many as fourteen or for as few as her ravenous family. The scent was out across the land. In the nine previous years when we had lived in Switzerland we had had exactly seven people to dinner. During Wendy's Mexican fiesta at Rossenarra, in the first four months we occupied the house, we fed sixty-eight. When Wendy reemigrated to Fort Worth, Texas, taking her son and her skillets with her, the invisible drawbridge was lifted; the crazing smells, wild colors, wonderful textures and astonishing tastes of Mexican cooking had disappeared from the land. Scarlet O'Gutiérrez had left Tara.

But, as technically soundly, intuitively, and painstakingly as Wendy does cook, and taking into consideration that she had lived for four years in Mexico (although only two of those as a housewife) and did know how the food should taste (generally), how it should look, and what might possibly not ever be included in it, she had produced the ninety-odd dishes for the sixty-eight people, cooking in areas she had never encountered before, and to all *non*-Mexicans she had triumph after triumph as she orchestrated two stoves, a deep freezer, two refrigerators, and a dishwashing machine.

You, too, can make an enchilada this quick, new, easy way, the banner headline might have said. Years ago Wendy spent two weeks and then one month perfecting her mastery of the chicken enchilada, but as time went on she was blithely running up masterpieces such as veal in pecan sauce or in green sauce, the tablecloth stainer, and endearments such as *pollo tabasqueño.* The pervasive fact about Mexican food is that it is not only for people who like to eat; it is, even more so if such a thing were possible, for people who like to cook.

4

There are yahoos who would disagree that there are only three basic, wholly developed systems of cooking in the world: the Indian/Chinese, the Mexican, and the French, and that all other cooking systems evolved from these or are dependent on these. Also, there is something called "international hotel cooking" which is *hors concours* because it does not resemble food systems or food or even papier-mâché representations of food. The "international" style was developed with a French culinary dictionary and by employing only Australian army mess sergeants as *chefs de cuisine.* All hotel chains offer this style. Possibly the worst ever tested was in the dining room of a hotel in Copenhagen which did not deign to offer *smørebrod* but presented an "Around the World" menu printed in eleven colors.

Then what is a "cuisine"?

If a cannibal boils a missionary and his wife that is not cuisine. But if he adds a touch of oregano and two onions he has made step one.

French cooking is the most vivid of all cuisines because the entire nation works day and night, with dedicated, proud interest, to keep it so. It would be hard for Australians or the Irish or Americans to grasp, but the French people have a total commitment to advancing the art of anything to do with food in the country. This interest extends from the people who produce the crops of grain, wine, and meat to the *chef de rang* who places the food before the diner. It has created a hagiology of cooks, the only peerage based upon art. It includes tens of thousands who write about it, legislate it, proselytize for it, and teach it the year round. The pantheon of great cooks and Amphitryons extends far back into French mists of time. They have believed in religion intermittently and when convenient. They believed in sex until the traffic problem became too great. They have a greater belief in money than the Swiss, but even that is as nothing compared with the thrilling devotion of their collective lives to food. Were they less hypocritical the *Jeu de Paume* would exhibit Haeberlin's spoons, Oliver's books, Troisgros's aprons, a sculpture of Bocuse's whisking wrist, Barrier's *toque blanche,* and copper utensils autographed by Outhier.

To accomplish what France has accomplished with food definitely takes the devotion of fifty million Frenchmen. French food does not remain the same. It not only changes, it improves when one would not believe it could. There is much talk of how French food is declining in quality and this is undoubtedly so. Deterioration leads change and decadence happens in areas where rigid tradition is the way. But if anyone could afford to eat from the kitchens of the great French cooks day after day one would observe no decline in quality, only that miracles were being passed before one's eyes. But the preparation of such food is so costly that "gastronomy of the highest order is no longer practiced by more than a tiny number of restaurateurs, perhaps as few as the great couturiers," the master Raymond Oliver has written. But, as *haute couture* is now used as the pattern for mass clothing, so is French cuisine, svelte in an inflated world, proof that the miracles of sensation and satisfaction can be passed along.

Oliver, the scholar and poet of food, wraps it up thusly: "In spite of all, French gastronomy based on cookery and wine not only survives but grows and indeed improves, as do all arts in a period of transition. The great crises of painting, whether impressionist, cubist, pointillist or abstract are simply stepping stones. . . . French cookery is analogous; it has had setbacks, periods of depression, moments of enthusiasm. . . . If the artist panders to contemporary taste . . . it simply adds to his experience, but to know what not to do is wisdom itself. . . . The game is a thrilling one, but one must learn the rules: how to eat and drink. A proper education in both these subjects can greatly intensify the pleasures they have to offer—perhaps even prove a revelation. What is the point of all of it? It is searching for a memory."

Throughout that statement runs the passion of a young culture. The Chinese and the Mexicans undoubtedly once had articulate advocates for the art of arts one thousand or four thousand years ago. After all this time they have, so many times, succumbed to pandering to the contemporary tastes, recovering, moving forward to new triumphs, then more decadences of pandering, and, worse, they have lost self-consciousness and have, at last, continued to produce the food as they had always produced—great dishes by the gifted cooks and *olla podrida* from the indifferent.

Systems of food preparation which have been patterned and codified until they become a tradition are formal cuisines. The Italian version of *In Which We Serve* revolves partially around 192 varieties of pasta. Americans eat tens of billions of sandwiches and other hand-held food each year and, in the Middle East they can tell you seventy-three ways to cook a lamb. After that, within the range of their raw materials, budgets, skills, and interest, they copy what the French have developed.

Persians complained about the meals of ancient Greece, saying there was never anything to eat after the flour course, but it could a Persian canard because the banquet was invented in Athens.

When imperial Rome took over, and the whole world moved to the left on the map, the Romans went to work with a vengeance to create a culinary tradition. But although the meals and gastronomy and gluttony of Lucullus and Apicius and Epicurus are often quoted, they were meals for the very few and they did not so much create a cuisine as they seemed to be willing to eat anything which didn't have nails in it: grasshoppers, ostriches, and dormice, for example. The Romans milled white flour, creating a vitamin deficiency which may account for Caligula, brought in spices from Asia and peaches from Persia, sauerkraut from Germany and haggis from Scotland, the last being sent back immediately. They imported fish from the far-off coasts packed in pots of honey; wines were suffused with spices, flowers, or drugs, so must have been pretty lousy wines, and the first hipsters were developed by the required method of eating, which was lying on one's side in a bedsheet propped up by an elbow or a slave.

Then the barbarians arrived from the north, and we all know what they eat: hamburgers, weiners, and beer.

But with it all, and considering that Lucullus' recipe which called for "the tongues of five thousand birds" also required that these birds "had been taught to say a few words," Italy had acquired a long head start on creating the first lasting system of food preparation in Europe. It was wildly adventurous food for a fraction of the people of the nation-empire, so it couldn't become a tradition any more than the people of the United States could be said to have a tradition of fox hunting because a few people in northern Virginia hunted foxes. However, the Venetians were great merchants who could keep expensive raw materials moving in. There were certainly accomplished cooks working in the palaces of the multiple Italian states. However, as with India, China, and Mexico, who were to be followed by France for the same rule, it is requisite if a culture is to establish a true cuisine that the raw materials of the prepared food be natively available and in quantity, quality, and variety, all produced at prices accessible to the greatest number of the people in predictable seasons, and not imported erratically across the world for a few.

Mainly, Italy is a long pile of rocks. Not much more than moss can grow on rocks (not that the French couldn't develop tasty dishes with this), so that, when the courtly train which accompanied fourteen-year-old Catherine de' Medici (she who ate with such a heavy fork to fill that young, strong stomach) included two accomplished cooks with their brigade of undercooks and assistants and the entire European concept of food eating was turned upside down, we are asked to believe. Catherine had come to France from Florence on October 20, 1533, a day which shall live long in napery, to marry the future Henry II, whose father, François I, was the last of the prodigious medieval trenchermen.

At once, it is continually suggested, France leaped out of an etiquette which required that chickens be ripped in half by the main strength of the diner then engorged, to Catherine's earthenware from Urbino, glass from Venice, enameled dishes by Bernard Palissy, and silver engraved by Benvenuto Cellini.

However, the French cook Guillaume Tisel, known as Taillevent, had written a distinguished cookbook *Le Viandier*, in 1375, 158 years before either Catherine or her cousin, Marie, wife of Henri IV, brought their Italian cooks from Florence. This presupposes that something was known in France about boiling an egg; the French do not stand still on questions of interest in food; food and wine are the French genius. Chances are there was a sort of exchange. The Italians taught the French how to make spumoni (with ice imported from Norway because it was cheaper than the ice which was to be had from the tops of the Swiss Alps), and the French taught the Italians nothing. High food runs in fashions. The Medici cooks influenced only the feeders in the great houses while the French cooks were working away at perfection for all. The food scholar Esther Aresty has established that the great leap forward happened 118 years after Catherine de' Medici arrived; in 1651, well into the reign of the Sun King. Mrs. Aresty writes: "The foundations for this change were laid by a single cookbook: *Le Cuisinier français* by François Pierre de la Varenne. . . . The cuisine that La Varenne suddenly unveiled must have been developing for sometime in noble French kitchens . . . until this time there had been no [cook]books other than the printed versions of the medieval *Le Viandier*. The cuisine revealed by La Varenne was much more delicate than that of the Italians."

Italian national cuisine is the unquestioned favorite of most of the people of the West. It produces wonderfully happy-making, stimulating, sensual food. But French cuisine is all that and high art as well. One could spend the rest of his days eating Italian food, a feat which would be impossible with French food for reasons of cost alone.

Italy's cooks and gardeners and feeders were the strong bridge over which Mexican raw materials rode into Europe from the New World. Waverley Root points out that the first tomatoes seen in Europe were yellow and about the size of a cherry (*pomo d'oro:* golden apple, although it could also have been *pomi di Mora* or apples of the Moors because the Spanish would have sold vines to Granada and North Africa first). It took nearly two centuries for the Italians to develop new, bigger, red varieties and to use the tomato regularly in cooking. The Italians ultimately took corn into their stomachs as if they were Aztec stomachs, and it is used today so widely in northern Italy as *polenta*, but it was slow catching on, almost two hundred years. The haricot beans which came from Mexico to Italy have descendants which live so deliciously today in the flasks in Florentine restaurants. The sweet red bell pepper and the stately turkey were instantly given honorary Italian citizenship.

The only important thing was that, because the Italians and the French pooled their knowledge and skills, the court, the bourgeoisie, and the masses at last began to enjoy eating, thus developing a cuisine at about six thousand years after the cuisine of Mexico had passed a similar point.

The Mexican food system is based on corn. Corn, through selection and scientific cultivation, is a man-made vegetable which loses all resemblance to the food we know when it is uncultivated and returns to its wild state. Corn feeds the people of Central America and western South America as far south as Peru. The Amerinds were more carnivorous, but corn was their basic food as well.

The Indian/Chinese cuisine is based on rice and feeds the people of Asia and East Africa. French cuisine is based upon wheat (and champagne) with meat. It dominates food-preparation systems in Europe, Eurasia, metropolitan South America, Australia, and North America. The people of Soochow and Coatzacoalcos would reject the relative blandness of French cooking.

The most accepted standard for the French food system, the *Guide Michelin,* divides the rating of all French restaurants into these thirds: food preparation; its service; the nature of the surroundings in which it is served. Further, French diners believe devoutly in the importance of these three parts for the construction of a great meal. Only French cuisine could have developed a diner such as Pierrette, third sister of Brillat-Savarin, who, at the age of ninety-nine years and ten months, according to Samuel Chamberlain, was dining in bed when she cried out to the family servant, "Quickly! Bring the dessert. I feel that I am going to give up the ghost!" The servant ran, but too late. "Madame had left the dessert behind and had gone on to take her coffee in another world." In that it was the Brillat-Savarin residence, the *Guide Michelin* would have awarded for the cuisine and ambiance, but would have faulted the service, making Pierrette's a two-star demise.

The Indian/Chinese cuisine has no such system of ready ratings because it began so early that other habits were formed and disciplines erected. It is dated with the beginnings of the Mohenjo-Daro civilization in the Indus valley, fifty-five hundred to six thousand years ago. This was a great civilization which had developed out of the southwestern Asiatic neolithic base but whose staple foods seem to have been wheat and barley, hulled in mortars as Mexicans crush corn to make *nixtamal* for tortillas.

Although China has had a culturally unified population for a longer continuous period than any other world culture, its civilization took shape much later than that of the Indus valley. China's culture became integrated early and, unlike others, never collapsed but continued its development ever since. The earliest Chinese date (based on an astronomical reference in the Book of History) is 2500 B.C. Chinese crops and cultivation methods were probably the best in the world prior to modern scientific agriculture. Contrasting with these dates of establishment, the Valley of Mexico was well-populated eight thousand years ago.

5

Under the modern calendar the Mexican cuisine dates from the early Mayan culture, which had highly evolved architecture, mathematics, a written language, and astronomy; had developed the zero figure before India; had set down rules for the game of basketball indicating that they had systematized their patterns of living, patterns which would have included a reticulated system of food production and preparation. Carbon 14 samples establish the Mayan civilization as being six thousand years old, approximately equal in time to the Indus valley culture and more than thirty-five hundred years older than the Chinese.

Mayan learning which survived the murder of their leaders by the conquistadores and the destruction of their written records by Diego de Landa, archbishop of Yucatán, in the plaza of Merida, is in the Dresden Codex, the record of Mayan knowledge which survived the Conquest. If the vital aspect of Chinese civilization is its unbroken continuity of integrated culture, it is worth noting that the Mayans had about five thousand years of building their civilization before the Spanish arrived.

Which came first: chicken or omelet? Are the Indo-Chinese cooking systems the basis of the exalted Mexican cuisine which they resemble? The Maya outlasted the Mohenjo-Daro culture by thousands of years, was far previous to the Chinese, and still managed to resemble the Sino-Japanese physically and by their cooking. Was there a steady interchange by sea, or across the Bering Strait, despite the width of the Pacific Ocean?

There is a vociferous group of amateur anthropologists who shore up various bars in Mexico City who acclaim that Mexico was originally populated and educated from Atlantis (lost or stolen), which was also responsible for the Egyptian civilization, coeval with the Indus valley, and that one of the trinity of ruling gods in the Mexican pantheon, Quetzalcoatl, was a castaway sailor from Atlantis who eventually made it back home to the Atlantis ruler, William Randolph Hearst, Sr., to assemble research teams, which then went back to Mexico to set up the Mayan culture. These partisans are known as the *American Weekly* school.

It is good that this is a book about Mexican food or serious ethnologists might be led astray. Mine is not a formal finding, gentlemen, really. It is merely a conjecture. However, I do reject the Atlantis linkage (including the Mexican derivation from Egyptian culture which was founded by Asiatic immigrants who imported wheat and barley plants with them). I favor the Milhous-Nixon formula, which was constructed by that famous family of sinologists that the Chinese and the Mexican cultures exchanged information and concepts over the millennia, including information on how best to stain a tablecloth. It would have called for an immeasurable series of quite long voyages, or even walks, but that is how our species is constructed. The distance between China and Mexico, with Thor Heyerdahl at the helm, was probably the same as the distance from earth to the moon for Neil Armstrong, and a great deal less expensive.

Except for their food basis of corn versus rice, both agricultural accidents, Mexican and Chinese cooking is closely related. China uses about eighty varieties of chiles, Mexico about ninety-two. Both cooking systems are boldly and totally sensual, having various exotic and subtle perfumes, incredible combinations of planned countertextures and vivid or delicate taste, according to the wishes of the artist who prepares the food. Both have contributed to the French cuisine through fixing attitudes within the "limitless" approach to cooking, and most certainly in terms of raw materials. The Tarascan Indians of western Michoacán, a Pacific state of Mexico, and the Mixtecos of that coast in the state of Oaxaca speak languages which sound like Chinese to the learned. They are also enclosed by what are essentially Chinese architectural forms, are philosophical and ceremonious, have been suitably warlike in phases, and look Chinese—which is a good thing because at this fascinating point it would have been a let-down had they looked Irish.

The cooking of France uses the products of nature in cosmetic forms closely identified with man. The cooking of Mexico and China uses the products of nature seemingly to become a part of nature. Until the Spanish Conquest, cattle and sheep were unknown to Mexico and pigs not yet domesticated. Even well after the Conquest, when the Spaniards had settled into what were the largest cattle ranches in history, the Mexicans remained crypto vegetarians who were largely indifferent to meat. These ranches were prodigious cattle factories. Years before the founding of any English colony on the northeast coast of the United States, these ranches were branding forty thousand head of new cattle a year on ranges as large as 1,843,746 acres having over two thousand employees, stocked with almost a million head of cattle, one hundred thousand sheep, fifty thousand goats, and twenty-five thousand horses—all on one ranch. However, the cattle weren't raised for meat. They couldn't be shipped, for want of refrigeration, so they went for hides into leather and the carcasses lay where they were skinned.

With the exception of fish, fowl, pork, and some deer, the Mexican cuisine was largely vegetable, as it remains, in a compromised way. China has ever been a cereal/vegetable/fruit cuisine, allowing fish and fowl. In Mexico, the ancient peoples worshiped gods of corn, earth, flowers, rain, salt, fire, cactus, sea snails, pulque, and the sun. When Mexicans ate the food which was clearly a gift from the gods, they sought and found a oneness with those gods. The original Aztec creator gods, Ometecuhtli and Omecíhuatl, the progenitors of all other gods, were known as the Lord and Lady of Sustenance. Despite the enormously varied uses to which France has put its cuisine (remembering the whacked-out expression on Brezhnev's face as they rode him around Paris between meals), even the French have not taken food that seriously.

The ancient Mexicans had ocean fish sent daily from the sea in tanks carried by runners in relay. Turkeys, pheasants, peccary, partridges, quail, ducks, doves, deer, and rabbits were abundant. Of these, turkey and deer were domesticated.

6

To the present, hunting for the pot is rewarding in Mexico. Wild turkey, called *guajolote* by the natives, and peccary, called *jabalí*, are found throughout the country. Large herds of collared peccary rove across the wilder areas of the Yucatán peninsula. The peccaries of Guerrero, the state which surrounds the great, groaning tables of the Familia Peña, at Acapulco, feed on orchids and papayas, *frangipani* and *jícama* instead of on commercial garbage, and are delivered, from forest to eater, in heady, preflavored state. Nutritionist Magnus Pyke states that the modern "scientific" argument that eating pork was forbidden to Arab and Jew alike because it can carry trichinosis is "not at all convincing." The connection between infected pork and trichinosis is a most recent discovery and the link between the two is not discernible without up-to-date equipment. Dr. Pyke's reason why the Middle East rejects pork on religious grounds is that pigs cannot be herded over long distances so they are not popular with nomadic people—who come to despise people who are able to keep and eat pigs.

In Mexico, thirty kinds of ducks and four kinds of geese are plentiful; ten varieties of quail, four sorts of pigeons, and five of doves. There is no area of Mexico where there isn't good dove shooting, and the legal bag is high. There are mule deer in the north and plenty of white-tailed deer throughout the country with the miniature, sixty-pound (adult) brocket deer to be found in the southern rain forests. A hunter can find all the bighorn sheep he can eat, in the Sonora mountains; then he can mail the extra parts to Miami to be stuffed and mounted as potency totems for the wall back home. The tapir, people say, is greatly prized as food. This six-hundred-pound relative of the horse lives in wiliest seclusion in the wildest parts of the rain forests in Chiapas. Detailed information on hunting one's own live Mexican food is authoritatively provided in *Wild Life in Mexico* by A. Starker Leopold.

Mexico City is a seafood capital, and relays of runners don't bring it in tanks any more. Planes and refrigerated trains bring it in from the Gulf, the Caribbean, and the Pacific. There is an astonishing variety: shrimp, oyster, tuna, moro crab, crawfish, baby octopus, pompano, and robalo are regulars. So is *caldo largo*, the bouillabaisse of Veracruz. *Huachinango*, the Pacific's red snapper, is the most popular Mexican restaurant fish. At the formidable Lincoln Restaurant, *huachinango* is served under a green *salsa Nicolás*, an elusively light velouté sauce made with parsley.

The republic has one unique fish, and few other countries (on this planet) can make that claim. It is *pescado blanco*, the translucent and delicate catch from Lake Pátzcuaro. It is a poor traveler and just about makes it to Mexico City. It should be eaten at lakeside, lest it leave its haunting flavor behind as it passes through the Valle del Bravo.

7

Because Mexican raw materials were simple and natural, the flavors and scents were given a wide, imaginative range by herbs and condiments. Who discovered chiles first and cultivated them to the extent of their present variety is not recorded and, surprisingly, no chile incumbent sits in the Mexican deity pantheon. People can take pulque or leave it alone. It has a soapy taste but the price is right. Pulque is in the pantheon. The pulque lobby knew where a few spirits were buried and they got their product across. The world would not be the same without chiles: sweet, or hot, or just supportive. In the gray world to the north a big deal is a dab of mustard on the side of the plate, where only a few crazies will fool around with stuff like horseradish or Cumberland sauce. Chiles are a pantheon in themselves, a substance at once starkly thermal, elegantly finishing, fresh, restorative, bang-on chemically healthy, superdigestive, and quite beautiful as objects in themselves. Combined forever in the Mexican national diet of corn and beans, chiles provide the necessary levels of vitamin B.

By the time of the Spanish Conquest, Mexican cooking had developed complementary sauces, as opposed to smother sauces, which were served beside main dishes and used to vary or complete vegetable and fruit flavors in dishes served in well over a thousand different ways. Bernal Díaz del Castillo, the most important conquistador because he recorded most of what he saw in his thrilling book, *The True History of the Conquest of New Spain,* wrote, in 1562, "For each meal over thirty different dishes were prepared by [Moctezuma's] cooks according to their ways and usages, and they placed small pottery braziers under the dishes so that they would not get cold. They prepared more than three hundred plates. . . . Moctezuma would sometimes go out with his chiefs and stewards and they would point out to him which dish was best."

Aaaiee—pink salmon with finely ground white onions and coarsely ground black pepper; golden soup; pale-green cucumber sauce covering *huachinango;* maroon beets, chinese-red tomatoes, black and foaming chocolate flavored with vanilla taken from the wild orchid, *thilxochitl,* and honey; an ivory sauce sparkling with chiles over the snowy breast of wild turkey; freckled, beige tortillas; pungent smells.

And what a gorgeous set of emperor, chiefs, and stewards, warriors, and women, priests, and counselors that was, as they sat to dine in an enormous room, one of many around a main patio of the palace; whose walls were hung with featherwork of exciting, delicate workmanship in spectacular colors. The nobles were arrayed in rich, dyed cotton wraps interlaced with rare feathers. Many wore the *quetzalalpitoal,* an ornament composed of tassels of feathers and gold which hung down the sides of the pale-amber faces from the tops of heads.

The warriors' hair was combed straight up into a high tuft from which fell bulky jewelry of many colors. All the men wore their false mustaches made of bright blue and green feathers, which had an epigamic function and hung from a hole in their nose partition. Around their necks were *chichiuitls* of golden shrimps or pearls. Some of the men carried long fans in many colors, or of brilliant white, and smoked tubes of aromatic tobacco. The women walked softly on bare feet, their purple-dyed hair falling to their waists, their teeth dyed pink, and their uncovered breasts tattooed with blue markings.

When the court was assembled, the emperor appeared, dressed in blue, the imperial color, with mantle and diadem. No Aztec looked directly at him; to do so was to die from the force of his brilliance. He moved through the awe to a platform raised three feet above the floor and sat upon an *ycpalli,* and golden screens were immediately slammed into place between him and the court; it was forbidden to see the emperor chew or swallow. He was a slender man of good height, with precious stones inserted into the holes in the sides of his nostrils. He was about forty years old. His hair was long enough to cover his ears. His scanty black beard was well shaped and thin. His face was somewhat long, but cheerful. The court ate even more cheerfully, for the emperor ran a tall stove, Mom was in the kitchen, and all were ever willing to be smothered in the sauces.

The "smother" sauces in Mexican cooking prior to the Conquest were developed to accommodate game and, much later, used to enhance the immigrant beef and lamb. The most widely used Mexican smother sauce is *mole*, from the Aztec: molli; now pronounced *mo*-lay. It appears in red, brown, black, and green. There are more different kinds of *mole* in Mexico than there are cheeses in France. Every cook seems to have a different notion. Our *mole* is made with five kinds of chiles; almonds, pecans, peanuts, avocados, raisins, peppercorns, cinnamon, cloves, and chocolate. It comprises twenty-seven ingredients and takes most of a day to make. There are simpler versions. All are deeply satisfying. In a precise sense, *mole* is not a smother sauce because the whole preparation, meat and sauce, is cooked together; on the plate *mole* smothers its roommate.

Another classical smother sauce is made with three variations: with pumpkin seeds (when it is called *pipián* sauce); with red tomatoes; or with green tomatoes. These must be the mildly flavored "apples of the Moors," called *tomates*, not the sort which are used in the Colossus of the North, called *jitomates*. *Pipián* is usually married to pork or duck, but it works seductively with chicken and rabbit. (Green *mole* is also paired with pork.)

Black, brown, and red *moles* were conceived, tried, tested again, evolved, and wholly developed over centuries, to belong with turkey. *Mole* is the great ceremonial dish of Mexico. Moctezuma had it offered at his banquet for the conquistadores, whom he had mistaken for gods—some gods.

If *mole* is for Sunday, the rest of the week in Mexican cooking is an intricately worked, enormous mural which uses three elements in its design. In the beginning, as it was in the middle, and as it will be in the end without end of Mexican food, there were chiles, corn, and beans.

Mexican soil has a pronounced influence on vegetable flavors, varying markedly from region to region. The soil has worked its wonders on ninety-two kinds of chiles. Corn, which is the staff of life, is the ancient cultivated plant of Mexico. Only in Peru was this wonder food brought to a more refined degree of crossbreeding and mutation. One cannot think of the food without thinking of corn and the myriad ways it is prepared.

When a sweet bell pepper is planted in the soil of Aguascalientes it changes to a sharp, concentrated aromatic flavor. It would taste sweet again if it were to be planted in Morelos and change color altogether in the soil of Guerrero, directly to the west. This is the soil which, by changing the character of the chiles, brought such sharp distinction to Mexican food.

When Mexican food is "hot," a condition which prevails in perhaps one third of the Mexican cuisine, chiles are the source of the heat. The sensation of burning which they produce to different degrees (and not all chiles are hot, either) comes from an alkaloid called capsicum which is sometimes used in pharmacies as a local counterirritant and gastric stimulant. It is not an illusion of burning. Break open a small chile with your hands and discover that it has thermal power which works on more than the mucous membrane. This heat is an aid to digestion because it generates a heavier flow of saliva to protect the epithelium of the tongue and sets off the flow of good gastric juices for the same reasons. In that way it is also an incomparable appetite stimulant.

The capsicums are a large family, greatly exceeding chiles in number. They are of the pod-pepper genus and, early on were misnamed "peppers," although they are in no way related to the classic peppercorn, which mounted so many expeditions in ancient and medieval times. There are many hundreds of capsicum varieties. The family includes paprika, sweet pepper flakes, chiles, red peppers, cayenne, and such blends as chile powder, curry powder, mixed pickling spice, and barbecue spice.

The capsicum chile is basic to the thermonutrient branch of Mexican cuisine. It comes in colors of torrid red, furious yellow, jungle green, fire orange, and umber brown. It can be hot enough to lift steam from the teeth of the most seasoned Mexican diner and make him reach for a tortilla, which acts like a blanket putting out flames. Woe betide the feeder who attempts to cool off with a chilled drink. It just happens that tortillas are the color of natural asbestos and have the skin texture of the stately crones of England. Tortillas are made from a dough of ground corn kernels soaked in lime water. The dough is slapped between the hands until it is shadow-thin, then grilled lightly. The sound of tortillas getting their faces slapped can be heard in the streets of any Mexican pueblo any morning, in the solid rhythm of a burro's walk.

There are visiting gringos who have said that any regular use of chiles will impair taste sensations because after one has become habituated to them all other tastes seem bland. On the other hand, gringos have little opportunity to become habituated to chiles, poor souls, and Mexicans, who do, won't have it any other way. We must cherish ever greater compassion for the chile-habituated Mexican who is required to visit the Colossus of the North, where he is served food which really impairs taste sensations because so frequently within the food of the Colossus no flavors exist.

The most widely used chiles in Mexico are: *serrano:* small, green and very hot, fresh or canned; *poblano:* large, wide, and green, not very hot, fresh; *jalapeño:* elongated, green or yellow, fresh or canned; *chipotle:* long, brown, used dry; *ancho:* red, used dry; *mulato:* dark red, almost brown, used dry; *pasilla:* very dark red, used dry; *pequín:* very small, red, very hot, canned; *cuaresmeño:* green, used fresh; *güero:* yellow, used fresh; *pimiento* (bell pepper): sweet, green or red. Others worth setting down because it pleasures one so much to say their names, even with a Tipperary accent: *chiltepiquín, habanero, xcatique, cuicateco, chilhuacle, mora,* and *tornachil.*

Including that array of chiles, every sound Mexican kitchen is stocked with: *jitomate, tomate de cáscara,* garlic, thyme, vanilla, oregano, laurel, chocolate, cinnamon, corn, Chinese parsley, *epazote,* and avocado.

Chiles are roasted and skinned, then cleaned by having the veins and seeds removed to reduce the piquancy, then soaked in hot water or milk. When the seeds are used for sauces they are toasted and ground. Señora Josefina Velázquez de León, director of the Culinary Arts Institute of Mexico City, advises that in countries beyond Mexico, when fresh, dry, or canned chiles which are required are not available, chile powder is a quite adequate substitute. In larger American cities *ancho, pasilla,* and *mulato* chiles are available in this form. One tablespoon of chile powder represents one whole chile.

However, Señora Judith Van Beuren, of La Fonda del Refugio, has this to say about ingredients obtainable outside Mexico, "The packing companies, freeze-cooks, and dehydrator wizards are necessarily having to experiment to try to approach more feasible versions of at least the unrelinquished, unrelinquishable favorites on the vast list of honored masterpieces of Mexican cuisine, and it is the most difficult assignment they have ever undertaken. Flavors change, of course, when fruits and vegetables are picked not yet ripe. Quality in all ingredients makes for high costs and the temptation is mostly not resisted to grind an old chile into powder and hop it up hot enough so that the falsification cannot be detected—nor any other taste."

8

He laughs at scars who has not felt a wound. It would be awful if the greatest practitioners took to using second-best or make-do materials. However, for the millions of cooks and chewers at home, the accepted way for spices and herbs has come to mean those in powdered form. Except in Mexico, we are all dependent upon those amazing racks upon racks of what seems to be most of the exotic spices in the world in powdered form. Cooking around the calendar in a city flat or well out in the country means one must depend upon those small boxes and bottles of spices from the Indies and New Spain as well as herbs which, in a different time of year, we might well have grown ourselves in a window box. To summon up the food we may suddenly recall with all nostalgic gluttony, we have to make do or do without. If 30 percent of the effect we think we remembered is lost this way, few of us know it. With all those powdered spices and herbs we are still far, far better off than the man who lives deep in the pampas of County Kilkenny, Ireland, who (too frequently) gets an unspeakable craving for a pastrami sannawitch *estilo* Stage Delicatessen in New York. They don't hardly ever make any of them things powdered and packaged. It's only a case of dream, baby, dream.

There is a sadness which is hardly tragedy, but perhaps a bit of amethyst *tristesse* about the way food books wish wistfully and collectively to bring so many aspects of the thrilling foods of the world between book covers, so that the gastronomically curious reader may feel that he understands what the people of other nations are eating and be rewarded, in the sense that interest is the key to life. In this eagerness and reaching for ingredients other than powdered spices, the books have been known to say words to the effect of: "If you can't get Parmesan cheese for the memorable *mostaccioli con manzo e melanzane,* by all means use processed store cheese (or condensed milk)." The only thing even close to such religious delusion is that expressed by the wife of a man who cannot stand eating finnan haddie, or even sitting near it. She adores finnan haddie. They have been married for thirty-six years and every time the smelly stuff appears at a restaurant table, she tries with all her heart to get him just to "taste" it.

Most people who are addicted to reading cookbooks rarely get to cook what is told about within them. They read them as an escape from television, the politicians, and the kind of novels we are writing nowadays. However, if one gallant woman or man should wish to re-create that which touches her or his memory/desire within books on Mexican/Icelandic/Bessarabian cooking, to prevent such tragedies as using processed cheese on the genius of *mostaccioli con manzo e melanzane,* I plead with you to write or telephone the nearest Mexican/Icelandic/Bessarabian consulate to ask in which shop in what adjacent large city the ingredients which you must have may be procured.

If you think Mexican/Icelandic/Bessarabian consuls on duty in foreign countries subsist on the food of those countries then you must weep for them. They are compelled to eat whatever it is they were fed from tadhood even if it isn't just like Mama made it. State in your letter that if it is possible that they themselves have found any of the following ingredients unobtainable so far from home, can they suggest what might be the best substitute. Enclose a stamped, self-addressed envelope and they will tell you. More than language, food is the most memorable sealer of friendship and rapport beyond extraordinarily beautiful women who are willing to fall in love with one madly for a suitably convenient (short) period.

However, the food books were written for you, and you might reason that, since you don't know how it should look, or smell, or taste, or feel anyhow, why should you get into an uproar when you know that you love processed cheese and/or condensed milk? That is a healthy attitude. It is essential to be very fond of what we like and, every now and then, call it something else.

9

The second basic Mexican food is corn. The Aztecs had four corn gods: one male, two female,
one serpent. During the month of Huey Tozoztli (the name for April, not a Southern politician or a Brown Panther), and especially during the pre-Easter carnival called Tlacaxipehualtizli, there were rites, serpentine dances, and skirmishes by ladies, which survive in the Mexican carnival and Easter fiestas today, especially among the Tarascans. Unlike other cereals, corn is attached to a cob instead of being covered by floral glumes, or chaff, as in other cereals. The entire ear is enclosed by modified leaf sheaths, which have the disadvantage of impeding grain dispersal; corn in the form we know today is dependent upon man's intervention for its continued survival. In agricultural economy corn is the most productive of all cereals. Record yields of wheat seldom exceed one hundred bushels an acre; the maximum yield of corn can be more than three hundred.

The earliest example of cultivated Indian corn comes from southern Mexico. R. S. MacNeish's large-scale field studies follow the using and sowing of wild corn in the valley of Tehuacán from 7200 to 5200 B.C. The tortilla, staple of staples, the corn crepe, which is Mexico's historic all-purpose food, is the envelope for almost everything Mexicans eat. A taco, which satisfies beyond dreams, is made either with a "soft" tortilla—the round, warm, super-thin, freckled, cooked but untoasted kind which has just been baked on a griddle—or with a "hard" tortilla, one which has been toasted roasted or fried. With the "soft" tortilla, the diner fills the envelope, at the table, with anything and everything on the table such as hot meat, refried beans, guacamole, *salsa picante*, and on and on, alone or in any combination, then rolls the flat pancake of the tortilla all around this delectable food, chewing and rolling his eyes ritualistically. If the taco is made of a hard tortilla, the packing is generally done in the kitchen with every variety of chewable (ordered in advance), then fried or roasted until the tortilla becomes a rigid tube around the filling. The side dish for this sort is usually guacamole—a blend of mashed avocados, onions, herbs, green chiles and tomatoes. Baugin's "Still Life with Water Biscuits," painted in 1630, seems to be a portrait of seven empty tacos.

The enchilada is achieved whenever sauce is poured over a hard taco to smother it and when the hot fat in which the tortilla was fried contains chile.

At this point the category fans out into a dazing congress of *antojitos*, theoretically little morsels which one eats as sort of hors d'oeuvre before the major tucking in. The problem is that people such as gringos cannot stop eating the damned things, and there are millions and millions in the world who believe that Mexican cuisine is confined solely to tacos, enchiladas, tamales, and chile con carne (a Chinese dish from Texas and the American Southwest). They most honestly believe this because they have never been able to stop eating at the *antojito* point. They gorge and nod, slurp, gorge, and nod. It is as though French cuisine had discovered a form of hors d'oeuvre which did not resemble a frigid, indifferent, northern blonde of a certain age and were able to match them with a society of pervs who then clung to the conviction that French cuisine was entirely represented by the likes of *barquettes à la cancalaise*, spinach *talmouses*, *cromeskquis*, or *oeufs mignon Beauharnais*.

The names of Mexican *antojitos* are all sensual taste words. If food could sweat this food would sweat. If food could copulate this food would go through its short life either pregnant or perpetually erect. Consider, *por favor, gorditas, dedos de charro, buñuelos, pambacito compuesto, bambasos, sopas, chalupas, tostadas, garnachas, chilaquiles, quesadillas, empanadas,* and *enrollados,* for openers. They represent the American food heaven; contrasting sandwiches which actually taste, touch, and make love to the teeth.

At breakfast one has tacos of refried beans. At the midday, the tacos can be made out of the pork in the *pozole,* from the stuffing of the bell pepper, from the bell pepper itself, the sauce that covered the bell pepper, or, absent-mindedly, one's own finger. *Chalupas* and *tostadas* are open-faced sandwiches using toasted tortillas. A *pambacito compuesto* is a loaf of bread cut in half, fried, then stuffed with sausage, potato, hot sauce, grated cheese and greens. *Gorditas de manteca* are tortillas a half centimeter thick whose borders have been pinched to seal in the flavor of the condiments, then spread with chopped or ground sausage and green *salsa picante*. *Garnachas* are corn tortillas of yet another sort spread with a thick cover of refried beans, vinegar-cured onions, fresh cheese, avocado, and tomato sauce. *Quesadillas* are fried, flaky horns holding melted cheese or pumpkin flowers. When the content is meat they are called *empanadas*, the Mexican twin of the Cornish pasty.

Tamales and *atole* are made with corn and are classical Mexican dishes, and (purely) tamales are in the *antojito* division, where dwell the right things at the right time. *Antojito* means whim or capricious desire, and I feel several of same rolling over me right now. According to rules (which gringos break, smash, and crash daily), *antojitos* are to be eaten at the third "light" meal of the day, served between 8 and 10 P.M. Tamales are made of cornmeal mixed with meat or chile, and occasionally herbs, wrapped in corn husks or, in the south, banana leaves. Tamales are eaten at breakfast or at the evening meal, but never at lunch.

Corn *atole* is a drink made with finely ground corn and milk, with baking soda, stick cinnamon, and either lemon or orange leaves added, to name one variety. *Atole* is a gruel made with corn in different combinations of fruit juices, milk, cream, or nuts. The basic batter may be prepared with boiled corn or cornstarch. Tamales and *atoles* go together like Elizabeth and Richard; like Nader and General Motors; like six and five. Tamales take time to make but they show up at home on all festive occasions and women vendors sell them in the city streets from large, covered clay pots which stand on charcoal braziers. Every state of Mexico has a different variety depending on the type of corn and on other ingredients native to the region. They may be made with tortilla *masa* or with cornmeal. But they are also made with fresh corn, potatoes, and rice flour, and filled with just about everything that otherwise can fit into a taco. There are sweet tamales made with combinations of *masa*, egg yolks, butter, coconut, cream, jellies, walnuts, and almonds which are dangerously addicting. The *tamal* is so incorruptibly Mexican that Wendy would not make one in Ireland, even though by using prepared cornmeal (*nixtamal* cornmeal), rice flour, canned tomato sauce, and chile powder, people who are badly hooked on tamales *can* make them outside Mexico. In lieu of corn husks or banana leaves one might wrap the tamale in the London *Times* for steaming.

Tamales made in Mexico contain as few as twenty-four ingredients. Short-cut tamales, made outside the republic, have as many as fourteen ingredients. It is better to wait until you get to Mexico to try tamales, but there is many a stubborn reader so we will include an extraterritorial method for making them in, say, a hotel room at Sacher's in Vienna.

Mexicans understand rice as the Chinese do. They fry it first in fat, then cook it in water. This keeps each grain of rice as separate from its neighbor as two pretty ladies who find themselves wearing identical dresses at a ball. In Mexico, it is not unusual to have two rice dishes at the same meal.

Frijoles, which are only beans in Boston, are boiled and served whole or boiled, then mashed with a fork and fried. I can smell them now. They are a beautiful deep maroon color on the plate and are called *frijoles refritos.* In natural state frijoles dress for dinner in black, yellow, brown, purple, red, pink, white, speckled and striped.

10

Those are the great staples: chiles, corn, rice to an extent, and beans. Other joys which come vividly to life on the Mexican stove are fowl, the indigenous vegetables, and fruit. The best Mexican fowl is better than first class—and that includes varieties of buzzard. The national dish of the country is turkey and has been for some thirty-seven hundred years before Plymouth Rock. Alexandre Dumas wrote incorrectly that the ancient Romans regarded turkey more as a curiosity than as a food. They did not regard it at all. Turkey did not exist in Europe until the Conquest. When turkey caught on in France, it was originally known as Indian hen—*poule d'Inde*—until it was corrupted and became *dinde, dindon.*

At La Fonda del Refugio (Liverpool Street, Mexico City), turkey *mole* served on Monday is begun on Friday, completed Sunday afternoon, then allowed to rest and intermarry its flavors until it is reheated the next day for serving.

All vegetables commonly eaten in the Colossus of the North are eaten in Mexico in addition to other vegetables which are memorably different. Consider *chayote* if you get that lucky. It is round, pale-green, and covered with bristles. It is boiled, peeled, sliced, then fried and—aieee! *Huazontle* is sort of wild broccoli. *Nopales* are the tenderest leaves of the branched cactus. These are dethorned and boiled or fried; or they are dethorned and eaten raw in salads, or prepared as chile and made into omelets. The *jícama* looks like a large, plump turnip. It has a cool, starchy taste and is very juicy. It is served raw in salads, or eaten raw in thick slices with red chiles and a sprinkling of orange juice. Mexican corn comes in eleven high-fashion colors like a Braniff 707. The most delicious of edible mushrooms is black (Ceres was the color coordinator here) and grows upon ears of orange-colored corn.

Cosmopolitan Mexico is in the tropics, 19¼° above the equator. Its fruits, therefore, are meaty, juicy, and of pronounced flavor. Mexican pineapples make other pineapples taste like novelty watch fobs. Mexico has normal-size bananas called *plátanos machos* and tiny ones, the size of a child's fingers, called *platanitos* or *dominquines*. There are also pink, orange, and peach-colored bananas. Iced *tuna*, which is the prickly pear, the fruit of the cactus, proves that Mexicans are willing to look in the oddest places for nourishment. A bowlful of delicious, fresh *quayabas*, guava apples, will perfume a room in fifty minutes.

It would be hopeless to try to describe the flavor of a fruit called *zapote*, which possesses what may be among the three greatest flavors in the world. *Zapote* grows on the chicle tree, from which bubble gum is made, from which Wrigley Field was built. Note carefully the part of the tree which the Mexicans permitted to be exported to the Colossus of the North. *Zapote* comes in black, brown, white, and yellow. Black *zapote*, served with a dab of sugar, some mashed banana, and a gurgle of sherry, served chilled, will have you cackling like Scrooge after his troubles were over.

Sadly, Mexican cheeses are not recommended, and one should also look hard at the milk and butter. In our joint time there, there was little effective pasteurization, and it is unlikely that the situation has suddenly changed in a few short years. Undulant fever appears with frequency and is said to be endemic in at least one large city area in the north. The disease is endemic in most countries of the world. It bends victims in half with rheumatism and ages people appallingly.

As for eating lettuce *or any raw vegetable or fruit which cannot be peeled*, it is emphatically out of the question in Mexico (and in parts of Switzerland and France). The use of human waste as fertilizer multiplies the peril of amebic dysentery. Further, you must drink bottled water when visiting any New World locale.

11

Let the term "bottled water" be a euphemism, however. Mexican beer is the peer of any Czech, Danish, or German beer. Carta Blanca and Superior are the lightest. Bohemia has a higher alcoholic content. Brand Dos XX (pronounced dos eck-ees) is beer as black as bock. The greatest of all black beers, from Yucatán, named León Negro, is hard to come by outside Mérida. Beer goes best with Mexican food. If it must be wine, stick with white, please.

Mexican wine is only fair. The reds are all ordinary. Noblejo, Capellanía, Rancho Viejo, Alamo, and Santo Tomás are recommended out of the choices at hand. It is very rare to stumble across bad wine anywhere. Some wines are merely light years ahead of others, but when only ordinary wine is available one is not only very happy to have it but it tastes much better every day at every meal.

We drank Santo Tomás white wines. Verdizo is a good Rhenish type with a cold, green cast. San Marcos Seco moves in the general direction of chablis, if you can find any chablis even if you know the general direczion. Among the rosé wines the most consistent are San Marcos Violeta and San Lorenzo Rosado, which is drier.

Mexican brandy is good. It has the Spanish-sherry smacking flavor rather than the floating-near-the-roof-of-the-cathedral overcast of French Cognac. The brands Parián and Evaristo are the driest. San Marcos Gran Reserva is mellow.

One should drink tequila if intent upon modifying the bottled-water gambit. Tequila isn't really the right choice to quench thirst, but it makes a good chaser for the bottled water. Aged tequila such as Tequila Pechuga Almendrado is a drink with which to read sonnets. Tequila is made from the blue agave cactus which grows in the state of Jalisco. If the drink does not come from there it is not tequila. Mescal, another agave distillation, comes from the state of Oaxaca. It is much the best to buy the most expensive tequila, which has been able to afford the reredistillation of alcohol esters, because the hang-overs are more amicable that way. Pay well but also be sure to read the label on the bottle. If the label does not state that the contents have been redistilled and aged, don't buy it.

At morning, mid-morning, afternoon, teatime, evening, and night, Mexicans drink chocolate, *estilo Moctezuma*. It is a different chocolate drink than perhaps would come to mind if you had not ever seen or tasted it. Beginning with the cacao bean, the effects which follow become contrapuntal in flavor, a multi-echeloned, combined, simple family gift from the whole array of Aztec food gods. The fruit of the cacao tree which grows on the subtropical slopes is a nut, and inedible. The man who swallowed the first oyster was as nothing to the man who figured out that something could be done with the nut of the cacao tree. It had to be toasted, then it had to be ground on a *hot* stone, where the random contrapuntal effects are arranged into chords so that the fugue may begin to play.

The stone on which the cocoa is ground is called a *metate*, and has been a part of all civilizations for twenty thousand years. While the grinding goes on the *chocolatl* is blended with sugar, cinnamon, and vanilla. The fire which burns under the *metate* renders the fats in the cocoa and ensures a smooth blend with the other ingredients. When almonds are added they create a rich foam when the chocolate boils. The cooling paste gets patted into small, round cakes, put into a bowl with water added, and beaten with twirlers called *molinillos* until it is all foam. Any other exotic flavors or aromatics as might occur to the maker during the twirling are added. It is served warm and foaming or cold and foaming. In the palace kitchens there were canals of very cold running spring water into which the *chocolatl* vessel could be lowered.

Another favored combination is a drink made with the cacao bean and *masa* (which is corn kernels ground directly into baking dough) blended with fresh, hot green peppers and *epazote*. Tarahumara Indian runners, who could keep going for two nights and three days, used combinations of cocoa-chile-*atole* blended, no doubt, with peyote as well, as their only fuel (which was called *pinole*). In the Aztec empire the cacao bean was reserved for royalty, the military nobility, and high priests, and in every way that combination of ground corn and chilled, flavored chocolate was the key to their safes. All cacao bean production had to be brought directly to the Aztec court. Cocoa was the legal tender of the time.

The Spanish Viceroy, Mancera, found his niche in Spanish history with his invention of a cup-and-saucer combination with which one could handle his chocolate while standing, sitting, kneeling, bowing, or dancing. *Mancerinas* are now made in Czecho-slovakia.

Drinks which accompany Mexican meals are made from flowers and spices. *Agua de Jamaica* is the drink that happens when boiling water is poured over Jamaica flowers and sweetened. *Tepache* is made of pineapple rind and water and is preferred when it has fermented a little. Cactus sap and water are allowed to ferment into *colonche*. *Sangrita*, used as a chilled chaser with tequila, is made of tomatoes, oranges, limes, an onion, *serrano* chiles, and sugar, with Tabasco sauce to taste.

Espuma is a Juchitan drink which combines hominy, toasted cocoa, dark brown sugar, and dried jasmine and hominy flowers. This is beaten in a jug of cold water until it foams. Only the foam is used to enhance the hot corn *atole* which has been prepared. *Rompope* is like a Christmas eggnog made with pure, forty-eight-proof alcohol. It can be bottled and kept for a long time. Pulque, the maguey beer, is often combined with almonds, sugar, and oranges, or melon, black peppercorns, and cinnamon, with prickly pears, or with oatmeal. *Horchata* is a drink made of melon seeds, limes, and sugar water. *Chicha* is made of corn kernels, barley, pineapple, orange juice, and cinnamon. Among the most popular of the *aguas frescas* sold by street vendors and restaurants are *tamarindo* and *chía*.

12

Breakfast in Mexico is almost always the same. *Frijoles refritos* are as fixed a part of it as *café au lait* is to the continental breakfast. The beans are eaten with tortillas and, usually, a four-egg omelet. In northern Mexico, the eggs may be fried or scrambled and served within a collar of green and red *tomates* and *serrano* chile.

Salsa mexicana, made with chiles, chopped onions, red tomatoes, oil, and vinegar, appears at every meal, including breakfast and all snacks. When Mexicans switch to bread as a change from tortillas, they have a wide choice of the closest thing to what used to be called *le bon pain de Paris.* Times have changed in the bread field, too. Only two countries in the world are making sound, crusty bread made out of flour, yeast, salt, and water: Ireland and Mexico. It seemed odd to me at first but the more I observed or remembered, I decided that the Irish and the Mexicans resemble each other in many ways. Bread is one. The subtracted sense of time is the other. A deep faith in the joys of talking for the sake of talking is a third.

Mexican bread, and most particularly Mexican rolls (the Irish bake execrable rolls), comes from rules set down by the French baker whom the Emperor Maximilian brought with him to Mexico in the 1860s.

Mexico is a leading coffee producer, so that, too, is a breakfast standard.

The main meal of the day is eaten at about 2 p.m. It is generally served in four courses: soup, main course, salad, then a sweet or fruit. Rice and *frijoles* will be served before or after the main course, but *are not counted as courses.*

Mexico offers some great fire soups. The greatest of these is called *pozole.* It is so explicitly warming and filling that it can be a main course. A sturdy example of a Mexican main course is *chiles en nogada,* which are sweet bell peppers stuffed with pork loin, garlic, tomatoes, parsley, vinegar, a clove, vanilla, saffron, nutmeg, almonds, raisins, capers, candied citrons, olives, and fat ham all rolled in flour, dipped in well-beaten eggs, and fried. Sieved walnuts, black peppercorns, and pomegranate seeds are sprinkled over this before serving. It is a new life; it will be a totally new perspective for you and permit you, at last and so rewardingly, to think in other categories.

The most representative Mexican salad is *nopalitos.* Its basis is the new green paddles of the nopal cactus. The spines are trimmed—¿*cómo no?*—but the vegetable is not washed, to make sure that the sticky sap does not drip out. Nopal cactus is an okralike vegetable, and to keep it from becoming too sticky, you put in a teaspoon of bicarbonate of soda, then cook it with a few scallions. In line with the cuisine's policy of providing the unexpected, this salad is sprinkled with Parmesan cheese before it is served.

As we have noted so voluptuously, the third meal of the day (and many snacks in between) is made up of those alluring, even wantonly seductive, *antojitos*.

Spanish food did not make a significant contribution to the food of Mexico beyond the *chorizo* sausage and a stew called *olla podrida*, except in the area of desserts. The crystallization of fruit is European. The uses of cow's milk, so essential to dessert making, may be said with majestic authority to be Spanish because there were no cows in the Western Hemisphere until the Spanish arrived. Almond sweets and fillings are Moorish fantasies and these have found finger-lickin' favor among Mexican sweet teeth. A dessert as simple as rice pudding or as famous, in Mexico, as *chongos zamoranos* require the mixture of milk, eggs, and granulated sugar and therefore are Spanish in origin. The Spanish could hardly be called popular in Mexico despite providing these small pleasures. In the entire country there is but one statue to Mexico's kindly, philanthropic, soft-hearted "discoverer" Hernando Cortés, and that stands in Cuernavaca. The heroically talented Mexican muralists, Rivera, Sequieros, and Orozco, journalists who reported on building walls for people who could not read, have cast Spaniards as forever to be a part of the murders, pillages, and book burnings of the Conquest and the slavery which followed it.

Capirotada is made with fried bread, sugar, cinnamon, nuts, and cheese, and there are other bread pastries, such as *membrillo*, but overall my memory of immortal *postres* rests upon the fruits which I had never heard of before nor have I seen since I left Mexico. And the greatest of these is *zapote*.

13

Mexico has a long honor roll of regional dishes around and throughout which one should waltz, spin, and rotate because their contrast is rich and dimensional. These dishes emerge from an enormous cornucopia which, today, is the fourth largest country in the world but which before kindly President Santa Anna took over also included all of Texas, New Mexico, Arizona, *and* California. Its area now is 761,600 square miles with a coastline on each side of 5728 miles. But there the resemblance to most other countries becomes less distinct. Mexico is mainly a culture resting on three altitude platforms which provide three entirely separate climates, flora and fauna, and a marked contrast in living styles. Example: the Mexicans of the highlands have a far more puritanical outlook, and observe the Spanish feudal concept of the inferiority of women, than the Mexicans of the *tierra caliente* on the coastal regions of these most tropical latitudes. There the relations between the sexes are natural and uninhibited and the sexual life as direct as a flung spear. If this sort of thing should appeal to you, perhaps I may be of some help. If you should move into the area and begin to make friends, the words *"Biizi gaade na ti bisidu"* mean gizza kiss in Zapotec and, if that seems to be working well it might be followed with *"Dezi biali raabe lazi dua diuzi guti naa pana kigi saga nayaa li,"* which translates into "Since I laid eyes on you I told my heart: let God strike me if we two don't get together." (No other food book offers a service like that.)

The coastal plains, from sea level to about three thousand feet, have a normal temperature of between 77° and 80° F. with a maximum of almost 120°. The balmy temperate zone, at elevations of three thousand to six thousand feet, lives within eternal springtime; the temperature, on the average, is 59°. Mexico City is in the "cool" zone, but the climate of Mexico City, before the terrible factories and the distressing traffic polluted the air of that immortal city in the sky, at 7200 feet, was the most perfect I have ever been blessed to live in.

Plant and animal life differs sharply with Mexico's varied climates and topography. The coastal plains are covered with a tropical rain forest, which merges into subtropical and temperate types as the plateau is ascended. In the northern states there is dry steppe vegetation, with desert flora over much of the area. Mexico is the world's largest Spanish-speaking community. There are at least thirteen different Indian language groups and many dialects with which to summon a waiter. The women of Mexico outnumber the men by only ninety-two thousand, most of them good cooks.

The dramatic contrasts in the geography and cultures produced a fascinating variety of regional food within that enormous country. The contrasts in regional food specialties in North America are fractional by comparison. The favored dish of Aguascalientes, where the status, all-gourmet Brenner garlic is grown to intoxicate all cuisines, is fried chicken. Aguascalientes is a small state in the center of the country which produces grains, wines, vegetables, and fruits, and has a strongly acid soil. Tabasco is a hot, jungle state; its outstanding regional dish is iguana, which tastes like frogs' legs, which taste like chicken so, you ask sensibly, why not just eat chicken and stay cool. Guerrero is a coastal state containing something called Acapulco. The bang-up, bang-on dish there is *ceviche*, which is raw pompano or haddock served with tomatoes, onions, avocados, limes, oil, vinegar, *serrano* chiles, oregano, and sweet bell pepper. Baja California offers a meaty sea-turtle soup. Campeche has octopus in its ink. Colima makes coconut candy. Jalisco gave the world the fire soup *pozole*, the firewater tequila, and a dainty leedle open-faced sandwich made with pigs' feet and beans called *tostadas estilo Guadalajara*. The specialty of Chihuahua, Mexico's great cattle state, is unaccountably a pork work called *mochomos*, but Sonora, the neighboring, rivaling cattle state remembers what is paying the bills and became famous for a dish made of beef tripes, intestines, and hoofs called *menudo*.

The chilly, tiny, arid central state of Tlaxcala celebrates lamb (with maguey and avocado leaves) called *barbacoa en mesiote*. The Mayans of Yucatán specialize in a delightful dish called *panuchos*, which is made with black beans, eggs and chicken breasts and thirteen other ingredients, and have a six-thousand-year-old recipe for suckling pig called *cochinita pibil* for the young man who wants to take his girl home to meet his ancestors.

We prefer the *mole negro* developed by the nuns of Oaxaca to the *mole poblano* invented by the nuns of Puebla. Both states also specialize in sweets as well as vying continually over who made *mole* first and who makes it best. Neither can make either claim and such nonsense should not be perpetuated. *Mole* is the Mexican ceremonial dish which the Aztecs were eating before St. Paul invented nuns. *Mole poblano* has twenty-two ingredients; *mole negro* has eighteen; but—aha!—*mole negro* has pork as well as turkey and twenty black *chilhuacle* chiles.

14

Mexican food should/must be cooked in clay utensils. Mexican food tastes better in clay utensils. However, in Ireland in the summertime we didn't have and couldn't buy clay utensils unless we had some made and we felt too busy to wait to have them made, so we cooked in large French and Danish casseroles and everything tasted better than great. Nonetheless, if you can obtain clay utensils these should be used, he harrumphed.

Cazuelas, or casseroles, vary in depth, shape, size and decoration. They serve as mixing bowls, saucepans, and baking dishes. *Ollas* are pots. *Jarros* are pitchers. These are customarily decorated with the names of the owners before being glazed.

The *metate* is the most basic tool in all the world's kitchens: the grinder. A *metate* exists on three legs, is tilted downward and has a place for a fire under it if it is the special *metate* used for grinding chocolate to render the oil or the cacao beans. The *metate* user works on her knees, rolling the long, cylindrical stone called a *metlapil* downward across the *metate* and the kernels of corn. Both *metate* and *metlapil* are chiseled out of black stone and roughed with a piece of flint to increase their grinding action.

The *molcajete* is a mortar in the form of a pitted, black-stone, three-legged bowl in which chiles, herbs, and other vegetables are pounded or mashed. The *tejolote* is the four-inch-long, two-inch-wide pestle.

The *comal* is a round, unglazed earthenware or iron sheet which is placed over flame and used to cook tortillas.

The *soplador* is a palm-leaf fan used to excite the fire in a charcoal brazier. These vary in size, color, and shape.

The *molinillo* is a carved wooden chocolate beater of unique shape which should be in museums as well as in kitchens as an example of art.

The advantage in the few work implements used in a Mexican kitchen is that one never has to wait for the arrival of the appliance-repair man.

Shall we begin?

THREE WAYS TO PEEL TOMATOES

TO PREPARE MEXICAN GREEN *Tomates*

TO PREPARE BELL PEPPERS

TO PREPARE DRIED CHILES

SUBSTITUTES FOR DRIED CHILES

CHILE PASTE

TO TOAST SESAME SEEDS

TO JUDGE WHEN LARD IS READY FOR FRYING

HOW TO MAKE TORTILLAS

HOW TO MAKE CHORIZO SAUSAGES

FRIJOLES REFRITOS

HOW TO COOK MEXICAN BEANS (*Frijoles Mexicanos*)

PURÉED BEANS ESTILO GENERAL ENRIQUE JORGE MOLINA

HOW TO COOK RICE

SOME MEXICAN SEASONINGS OTHER THAN CHILE

basic mexican cooking

THREE WAYS TO PEEL TOMATOES

1. Roast over an open flame until the skin bursts, then peel the skin off.
2. Put in boiling water for a minute or two.
3. Put on an ungreased skillet over heat and keep turning until skin bursts.

Halve the tomatoes and scoop out the seeds.

TO PREPARE MEXICAN GREEN *TOMATES*

Remove the outer membrane and boil the *tomates* until they are soft, but do not overcook or they will burst. Mash, chop, or puree. The green *tomate* is not an unripe red tomato at all. It is inedible unless cooked.

TO PREPARE BELL PEPPERS

Singe the peppers directly over a flame, turning them gradually, or under a grill if you use an electric stove. When the peppers have been lightly toasted, wrap them in a damp cloth to "sweat" for ½ hour; then they may be peeled with little effort. Slit the peppers lengthwise and remove the veins and seeds. Rinse and soak in 1 quart water, which contains a teaspoon of salt, for 20 minutes before using.

TO PREPARE DRIED CHILES

Regardless of variety, pull off the stems and the core. Remove the veins and the seeds (reserving as many seeds as your inner heat-control apparatus will desire, for it is the seeds which provide the fire). Wash the chiles slightly in cold water, chop them into rough pieces, and soak these in 1 cup hot water to every 6 chiles. It is all very well to use your *metate*, if you have one, but otherwise grind them with the water they were soaked in (and some seeds) in an electric blender.

SUBSTITUTES FOR DRIED CHILES

Ancho, pasilla, and *mulato* chiles are not always available outside Mexico—perhaps the understatement of the year. However, all three varieties are sold in powdered form with no additions of other spices. These specific chile powders, designated by their names, are not to be confused with the generic "chile powder," which is a blend of unidentified chiles masked with herbs and spices.

When *ancho, pasilla,* or *mulato* chile powder is to be used it is mixed with flour and water and the resultant paste can be used in any of the recipes in which chiles are called for.

CHILE PASTE

Blend ingredients thoroughly. The mixture must boil briefly to season evenly. The tablespoon of chile powder is the equivalent of 1 chile. Be sure to multiply the quantity in proportion to the number of chiles required by each recipe.

1 tablespoon chile powder
1 teaspoon all-purpose flour
1 tablespoon cold water

TO TOAST SESAME SEEDS

Scatter them thinly in a baking dish and place in a 350° oven for 20 minutes, or sprinkle into a dry skillet and toast until lightly browned.

TO JUDGE WHEN LARD IS READY FOR FRYING

Heat the lard in a skillet until it bubbles vigorously around an inserted wooden spoon. The fried food will then be prepared without absorbing the flavor of raw lard.

HOW TO MAKE TORTILLAS

Mix the ingredients to make soft dough. Divide the dough into portions the size of Ping-Pong balls and place them, one at a time, on a tortilla press between waxed paper. Press to form a thin round crepe about the size of a pancake. If the tortilla sticks to the press, make the dough drier by adding more flour. If the tortilla is crumbly, add water to the dough. Cook the tortillas on an ungreased heavy iron skillet over medium heat until lightly browned on both sides.

Wrap the tortillas in a damp cloth, stacked like quires, and keep in a low oven until ready to use. If they should get dry, pat them several times each between dampened hands.

2 cups *masa harina*
1 teaspoon salt
1¼ cups water

HOW TO MAKE CHORIZO SAUSAGES

You can buy these already made in Latin American and Spanish food shops. However, if you can't buy them prefab they are worth making as they add importantly to many dishes. Besides, you get to enjoy them twice. The smell of them abuilding makes a house a home.

Mix all ingredients *very* thoroughly and stuff into sausage casing, tying it off into 4-inch links. Hang the sausage string to aerate for 24 hours before beginning to use. *Chorizo* sausages may hang indefinitely in a cool, airy place.

Grind together:
2 pounds pork (any cut)
1 onion
6 cloves garlic

To this add:
4 ounces chile powder
4 ounces paprika
1 cup cider vinegar
¼ cup rum or cognac
1 teaspoon black pepper
1 teaspoon ground cinnamon
¼ teaspoon ground cloves
10 ounces pork fat, finely diced
1 teaspoon salt

FRIJOLES REFRITOS

This is something we find ourselves longing for the way we long for New York delicatessen sour pickles and freshly made Swiss *saucisses de veau,* English syllabub, and chili con carne. Refritos means refried, but these are really beans already cooked, as below, which are then fried. Nothing quite accommodates a tortilla like *frijoles refritos,* and we recommend that a little Tabasco sauce be added.

Wash the beans in running water, removing foreign matter. Let them soak for 8 hours in enough water to cover. Drain.

Cook the beans with the onion in covering water over low heat. When the skins begin to wrinkle, add 1 tablespoon of the lard and the *epazote* and cover the pot. As the liquid is absorbed add more hot water. After 3½ hours add the salt. Cook another ½ hour and remove the *epazote.*

Mash the beans with a fork, or put half the beans in an electric blender and mash only half of them. Heat lard in a skillet and add the mashed beans. Stir and turn the beans occasionally until they are heavy and thick. Sprinkle with the grated cheese before serving.

1 cup pink, red, or black kidney beans
4 quarts water
1 onion
1 sprig *epazote,* if available*
6 tablespoons lard
1½ tablespoons salt
½ cup grated Parmesan cheese

* It should be noted that while *epazote* adds much to the flavor of the beans, it produces a horrible smell while cooking. If you are forewarned you will not be turned off.

HOW TO COOK MEXICAN BEANS

Frijoles Mexicanos

Clean the beans in running water, removing all foreign matter. Soak them for 8 hours before cooking. Cover the beans and the onion with water and bring to a boil. A flameproof earthenware pot is best. When the skins of the beans begin to wrinkle add 1 tablespoon of the lard and the *epazote*. Simmer the beans slowly in a covered pot and as the liquid is absorbed add more hot water. After 3½ hours, when the beans are almost done, add the salt and cook on until the beans are very soft. Strain the broth into a large bowl, mash 3 tablespoons of the beans, and stir these into the broth. Cook the remainder of the beans in remaining tablespoon of lard, strain the bean stock again, and pour it over the beans. Season with salt and pepper and simmer until very thick, about 1 hour.

1 cup pink, red, or black kidney beans
1 onion
4 quarts water
2 tablespoons lard
1 sprig *epazote,* if available
1½ teaspoons salt
Salt and pepper to taste

PUREED BEANS ESTILO GENERAL ENRIQUE JORGE MOLINA

Cook the beans as for *Frijoles Mexicanos* to the point where they are just soft. Drain off 1 cup of the bean broth and discard. Let the beans cool slightly, then puree them in an electric blender with the remaining broth and with the Cheddar cheese. Add the onion, eggs, and butter to the puree and season with salt and pepper.

Put the puree in a baking dish and bake for 15 minutes in a 350° oven. Sprinkle with grated Parmesan cheese and serve hot.

1 cup red beans
6 ounces Cheddar cheese
1 medium onion, finely chopped
2 eggs, beaten
3 tablespoons melted butter
Salt and pepper to taste
½ cup grated Parmesan cheese

HOW TO COOK RICE

Soak the rice in hot water for 15 minutes. Rinse it until the water runs clear and drain well. Fry the rice in the hot corn oil with the onion until the rice and the onion are golden. Pour off the excess oil and add the hot water. Simmer until the liquid is absorbed by the rice. Add the milk and the salt. Cover and simmer over low heat until almost dry—about 15 minutes. Take off heat and add butter.

1 cup rice
½ cup corn oil
1 medium onion, chopped
½ cup hot water
2 cups milk
1 tablespoon salt
4 tablespoons butter

SOME MEXICAN SEASONINGS
OTHER THAN CHILE

ACHIOTE (annatto), a tree seed often used in Yucatán cooking. The pulp of the seed gives food a golden color and adds a delicate flavor.

AJO (garlic), but certainly.

AJONJOLÍ (sesame seeds), an oily seed used in sauces, baking, and desserts. It is a splendid garnish. It has a nutty flavor and is high in protein.

ANÍS (anise), aromatic and flavorsome. It tastes like licorice but is a member of the parsley family.

AZAFRÁN (saffron), golden colored, golden cost: The world's most costly seasoning.

CANELA (cinnamon), versatile, used in a wide range from meat to desserts.

CHILES, beyond all categories, the staff of life, the flame of the game.

CILANTRO (coriander, Chinese parsley), widely used in Mexico.

CLAVO (clove), highly scented and pungent, used whole or ground.

COMINO (cumin) is not to be confused with its caraway cousin, which is called cumin in Europe, though both are parsley forms. *Comino* is pungently Mexican.

JENJIBRE (ginger), on loan from the Orient for four centuries, gives sharp, exciting taste.

LAUREL (bay leaf).

MARJORAM is sometimes mistakenly called oregano in Mexican food supports. They are both of the mint family but marjoram is sweeter, more delicate, and has a special scent.

NUEZ MOSCADA (nutmeg), whose flavor is sweet with mellow, spicy undertones; widely used across the card.

OREGANO, also known as Mexican sage. It has a full, assertive, and pleasantly bitter flavor.

PEPITAS (pumpkin seeds) has a distinct yet subtle flavor. It is used for *moles,* sauces, flour, and desserts.

PIMIENTA DE CAYENNE (cayenne) is the hottest pepper. Often more than one variety of capsicum is used to make cayenne.

PIMIENTA (pepper): both black and white are used. Pepper compliments other spices.

PIÑON (pine nuts), a subtly flavored, small oil nut used for sauces and sweets.

TOMILLO (thyme), a moderately potent herb used for fish, poultry, and sauces.

STAGE TWO

a rehearsal

In *Kitchen Book,* a delicious account of life around the stoves in the great, old, European hotels, Nicholas Freeling, novelist and long-time professional cook, states flatly: "You cannot teach cooking out of a book any more than you can carpentry. No two stoves, frying pans, ovens—come to that no two cooks—are the same. No good writer on food gives formal recipes."

He must have meant professionally prepared French food, high cooking at that, of course. Or perhaps the food of any country in which the feeder resides and can watch native cooks. If Mr. Freeling did not leave Europe he could not learn how to prepare ancient Mexican cuisine unless he was taught from a book—the way my wife's mother learned carpentry, because Mexican restaurants in Europe are abominable. In all of them peculiar dishes bearing Spanish nouns with *-ita* at the end (and probably—ugh—curry powder within), are sold as if we were all in central Durango.

Even for such an experienced professional cook as Mr. Freeling, an account of the food which contained recipes and their methods of production would be essential outside Mexico. By reading this book, some recipe-taught, book-larnin' cooks might be luckier than others, but all of them can be successful if they complete the rituals which follow because, essentially, Mexican cooking is not difficult.

Interest is the key. As with life, so it is with Mexican cooking—interest is the clue.

However, it can do nothing but good if a few of the less complicated pieces for the stove are shown in this section, to be cooked now, on which to practice before moving on to Benito-Juárez Schumann's *"Warum?"* Start with one or a combination of these dishes and cook your way to confidence. Confidence is the trampoline which throws the achievements of the new Mexican cook even higher. Practice makes. Therefore, what follows will be a list of Mexican dishes which are simpler to prepare and cook than others. If you will choose a menu of two or three of these and cook each of them two or three times—not on the same day, of course, but perhaps during a month, until you gain confidence in how each one is put together—you will be all the more ready to take on any of the more complicated dishes which follow.

Keep remembering: Mexican food is not difficult, but to deliver the results expected it does require more time in the kitchen than might be spent on the preparation of other food. Ay, there's the grub! Mexican cooking means work and time in the kitchen. One must allow plenty of time so that the enjoyment of cooking it is not diminished.

And a good nose is requisite also, to smell out work for the other senses, as someone wrote into *The Winter's Tale.*

Stay loose. Choose a menu from the list that follows, then turn to STAGE III for instructions as to how to operate the time machine, that stove which will transport you back 6000 years.

SOUP	*La Mejor Sopa de Elote* (Best Corn Soup)
ANTOJITO	*Tostadas de Frijol* (Especially if canned *frijoles* are used), or *Chilaquiles*
FISH	*Aguacates Rellenos con Camarones* (Avocado stuffed with Shrimp) or *Jaiba Veracruzana* (Vera Cruz Crab)
CHICKEN	*Pollo con Salsa de Piñones* (Chicken in Pine-Nut Sauce)
MEAT	Beef Stew
VEGETABLE	*Torta de Papas con Limón* (Lemon-potato Cake)
SALAD	*Ensalada de Juárez o Ensalada de Aguacate* (Juárez Salad or Avocado Salad)
RICE	Sesame Rice Mirza
DESSERT	*Macedonia*

"Why should the Marquis de Cussy wage war on soup? I cannot understand a dinner without it."

Last words of M. A. Carême,
chief cook to the English court, the Russian
court, and Baron Rothschild.

mexican recipes

SOUPS *SOPAS*

SWEET-POTATO SOUP
Sopa de Camote, Hildita Marton

MACARONI AND SPINACH SOUP
Sopa de Macarrones con Espinacas

TORTILLA SOUP
Sopa de Tortilla

FIRE SOUP JALISCO
Pozole Estilo Jalisco

AVOCADO SOUP
Sopa de Aguacate

BEST CORN SOUP
La Mejor Sopa de Elote

CHICK-PEA SOUP
Sopa de Garbanzos

BEAN SOUP
Sopa de Frijoles

MEXICAN SOUP
Sopa Mexicana

ZUCCHINI AND TURKEY SOUP
Sopa de Calabaza y Guajolote

CARROT SOUP
Sopa de Zanahorias

BEEF BROTH
Sopa Sencilla

VERMICELLI SOUP
Sopa de Fideos

SWEET-POTATO SOUP

Sopa de Camote, Hildita Marton

Melt the butter in a skillet and sauté the onion, *cilantro* or parsley, tomatoes, and sweet potatoes for 8 minutes. Put the sautéed ingredients in a blender with the milk and puree. Pour the puree into the beef stock and simmer for 20 minutes. Season with salt and pepper. Add the cream just before serving. Garnish with grated coconut.

3 tablespoons butter
1 onion, minced
2 tablespoons chopped *cilantro* or parsley
3 medium tomatoes, peeled, seeded, and chopped
½ pound sweet potatoes, peeled, cooked, and chopped
¾ cup milk
1 quart beef stock or consommé
Salt and pepper to taste
¼ cup heavy cream
3 tablespoons grated coconut (optional)

MACARONI AND SPINACH SOUP

Sopa de Macarrones con Espinacas

Cook the macaroni in 6 quarts boiling water for 5 minutes, then drain. Fry the bacon, onion, and garlic in lard until lightly browned. Add tomatoes and fry for 3 minutes. Add this sautéed mixture to the stock in a large pot and boil 5 minutes. Add macaroni and spinach. Salt and pepper to taste. Simmer 10 minutes. Serve garnished with grated cheese.

8 ounces elbow macaroni
3 slices lean bacon, chopped
2 tablespoons finely chopped onion
2 cloves garlic, finely chopped
1 tablespoon lard or olive oil
3 medium tomatoes, peeled, seeded, and chopped
1½ quarts stock or beef consommé
1 cup cooked and chopped spinach
Salt and pepper to taste
Grated cheese

TORTILLA SOUP

Sopa de Tortilla

Cut the tortillas into strips the width of your finger. Fry them in hot oil and lard until crisp. Remove and drain on paper towels. Fry the onion and tomato puree in remaining oil over lower heat for 5 minutes. Add this and the tortillas to boiling chicken broth together with the coriander. Simmer for ½ hour. Put grated cheese in each soup bowl and pour the hot soup over it.

9 tortillas
¼ cup corn oil
2 tablespoons lard
1 onion, chopped
⅓ cup tomato puree
2 quarts chicken broth
1 tablespoon chopped fresh coriander
1½ cups grated Monterey Jack cheese

FIRE SOUP JALISCO

Pozole Estilo Jalisco

Cook the pig's foot with all the garlic in salted water to cover for 2½ hours. Remove and discard the foot. Add the chicken and pork with chicken stock or water, cover, and simmer for 1 hour. Strain the broth. Skin and bone the chicken and return the lumps of chicken to the broth along with the pork. Add the hominy and chile powder and cook 20 additional minutes. Season with salt and pepper. Serve the broth with the meat, garnished with shredded lettuce, chopped onion, radishes, red pepper flakes, oregano, and lime wedges. *Pozole* is a complete meal.

1 pig's foot
1 entire garlic bud, peeled
1 chicken, cut into serving pieces
1 pound pork loin, cut into cubes
1 quart chicken stock or water
4 cups cooked or canned hominy or *garbanzos*
2 tablespoons chile powder
Salt and pepper to taste
1 small head Boston lettuce, shredded
1 onion, chopped
1 bunch radishes, sliced
Red pepper flakes to taste
Oregano to taste
2 limes or lemons, cut into quarters

AVOCADO SOUP

Sopa de Aguacate

Sauté the flour in the butter and add the chicken stock before the flour browns. Simmer until it thickens slightly. Add salt and pepper and remove. Mash avocados with the cream, add onion juice, and pour over hot soup. Fry tortilla squares in lard and add to hot soup. Serve at once.

2 tablespoons flour
4 tablespoons butter
2 quarts chicken stock
Salt and pepper to taste
5 large avocados, peeled and pitted
½ cup cream
½ teaspoon onion juice
2 tortillas, cut in squares
2 tablespoons lard

BEST CORN SOUP

La Mejor Sopa de Elote

Sauté chopped onion in butter until soft. Put in blender with corn and pimientos and puree. Mix with consommé in a saucepan and heat through. Add salt and pepper. Just before serving stir in the cream. Do not allow to boil.

1 onion, chopped
2 tablespoons butter
2 cups cooked corn kernels
2 canned pimientos, roughly chopped
4 cups beef consommé
Salt and pepper to taste
¾ cup heavy cream

CHICK-PEA SOUP

Sopa de Garbanzos

Put the chick-peas in a blender with ¼ cup of the stock and puree. Add the puree to the stock and cook for 15 minutes. Fry the bacon; set aside. Fry garlic and onions in same pan with the lard. Meanwhile, chop bacon. When onion is soft add tomatoes and cook 3 more minutes. Mix this together with chick-peas and stock. Strain. Add chopped bacon and salt and pepper. Serve very hot.

1½ cups cooked or canned chick-peas
1½ quarts stock
½ pound lean bacon
2 cloves garlic, chopped
2 onions, chopped
2 tablespoons lard
2 medium tomatoes, chopped
Salt and pepper to taste

BEAN SOUP

Sopa de Frijoles

Soak the beans overnight in 6 cups water. Gradually bring the beans to a boil over low heat and cook slowly. Fry the pork in lard or corn oil until browned, then cut the pork into small cubes. Add these to the boiling beans with the onions, garlic, cloves, oregano, cayenne pepper, and bay leaves. Cover and simmer for 4½ to 5 hours. Add salt ½ hour before soup is done. Let the soup cool. Pour the soup into a blender, filling it half full at a time. Puree all the soup. Reheat for serving and add the lime juice (Rose's unsweetened lime juice may be used). Garnish with radish slices.

1 pound small dark-red or black beans
6 cups water
1 pound pork, sliced and fried
1 tablespoon lard or corn oil
2 onions, chopped
1 clove garlic
3 cloves
1 teaspoon oregano
½ teaspoon cayenne pepper
2 bay leaves
Salt to taste
2 tablespoons lime juice
Radish slices

MEXICAN SOUP

Sopa Mexicana

Cook the chicken breasts in 1½ quarts water with onion, celery, and 1 teaspoon salt. When the chicken is tender, strain the broth. Skin and bone the chicken and cut into big chunks. Sauté the pureed tomatoes with the grated onion and ½ teaspoon of salt, in lard. Put the carrots in the broth to simmer. When the carrots have been cooking 10 minutes, add the zucchini. Add the tomato puree and cook 10 more minutes. Take the soup off the heat, put in the chicken and stir in the cream. Lay strips of avocado in the soup dishes, fill with soup and serve *jalapeños* on the side.

2 chicken breasts
1 onion
1 stalk celery
1 teaspoon salt
4 medium tomatoes, peeled, seeded, and pureed
1 tablespoon grated onion
½ teaspoon salt
1 tablespoon lard
2 medium carrots, scraped and sliced
2 medium zucchini, cut lengthwise and sliced
¼ cup light cream
1 avocado, cut into strips
2 *jalapeño* chiles, sliced and seeded (optional)

ZUCCHINI AND TURKEY SOUP

Sopa de Calabaza y Guajolote

Put the cooked zucchini pieces with the chopped onion and ½ cup of the stock in a blender and puree. Add the puree to the remaining stock with the corn flour diluted in a little water; add salt and cook slowly for 40 minutes. Pour in the cream just before serving.

1 pound zucchini, cooked and sliced
1 large onion, chopped
6 cups turkey stock
2 teaspoons corn flour
1 teaspoon salt
½ cup light cream

CARROT SOUP

Sopa de Zanahorias

Cook the carrots in water with sugar and salt for 15 minutes. Drain carrots and grind with 1 cup of the milk in a blender until smooth. Pour into a pot with another cup of milk. In a saucepan melt the butter, and stir in the flour until brown. Gradually add the remaining milk and, while it simmers, stir for 5 minutes. Combine with the carrot mixture, add cream, and stir. Season to taste with nutmeg, salt, and pepper.

6 large carrots, scraped and halved
1 teaspoon sugar
1 teaspoon salt
1 quart milk
2 tablespoons butter
2 tablespoons flour
⅓ cup heavy cream
Dash of nutmeg
Salt and pepper to taste

BEEF BROTH

Sopa Sencilla

Put all the ingredients except the rice and avocado in a pot, bring to a boil, then simmer for 2 hours. Drain the broth and reserve the cubed beef. Skim away any fat from the broth, heat to boiling, then add the rice and lower the heat. Simmer for ½ hour. Shred the beef cubes and return to the soup. Lay avocado strips in the soup dishes and pour the soup over them.

1 big marrow bone
½ pound beef, cubed
1 clove garlic
1 small onion
⅛ teaspoon cumin
2 teaspoons salt
½ teaspoon pepper
2 medium tomatoes, peeled and chopped
1½ quarts water
1⅓ cups of rice
1 avocado cut into strips

VERMICELLI SOUP

Sopa de Fideos

Fry the vermicelli in hot oil, stirring, until golden brown. Remove and set aside. Put tomatoes, onion, and garlic in a blender and puree. Fry this in 1 tablespoon of the oil for 3 minutes. Combine all the ingredients in boiling broth and cook for 10 minutes.

½ pound vermicelli
¼ cup corn oil
2 tomatoes, peeled and chopped
1 small onion, roughly chopped
1 clove garlic, sliced
1½ quarts chicken broth
Salt and pepper to taste

ANTOJITOS

"Better be early than late at the feeding place in a world full of hungry creatures."

Karl von Frisch
Professor, University of Munich

Chilaquiles Rojos con Pollo

Chilaquiles Verdes

Empanadas

Enchiladas de Mole

Enchiladas Estilo Jalisco

Gorditas

Papatzul

Quesadillas con Tuétano

Tacos de Mochamos

Tacos de Pollo

Tortas de Jamón y Queso

Tostadas de Frijol

Tostadas de Pollo

Tostadas Tapatías

Tostaditas

Totopos

Tamales de Pollo al Estilo de Señora Keifetz

CHILAQUILES ROJOS CON POLLO

Cut the tortillas into strips ¾ inch wide and fry in all but 1 tablespoon of the hot oil or lard; do not brown. Drain on paper towels. Put the tomatoes, chiles, onion, garlic, *epazote*, and salt in a blender with ¼ cup of the chicken stock and blend into a smooth puree. Sauté the puree in remaining tablespoon of lard for 5 minutes, stirring. In a well-greased casserole place a layer of fried tortilla strips, a layer of tomato sauce, some of the cream, and half of the chicken. Make another layer and top with a layer of tortilla. Pour over any remaining sauce and remaining ½ cup chicken stock. Sprinkle on the grated cheese and bake in a moderate oven for 1½ hours.

25 tortillas
1 cup oil or lard
1 pound tomatoes, quartered
4 *serrano* chiles
Onion
1 clove garlic, chopped
2 *epazote* leaves (if available)
½ teaspoon salt
¾ cup chicken stock
1 cup heavy cream
2 cooked chicken breasts, cut into pieces
¾ cup grated cheese

CHILAQUILES VERDES

Cut the tortillas into strips ¾ inch wide and fry in all but 1 tablespoon of the oil or lard; do not brown. Drain on paper towels. Put the tomatoes, chiles, onion, garlic, *epazote*, coriander, and salt in a blender to make a puree. Sauté the puree in remaining tablespoon of lard for 5 minutes, stirring. In a well-greased casserole place a layer of the fried tortillas strips, a layer of grated cheese, a layer of sauce. Make 2 layers each, then top with tortilla strips. Pour over any remaining sauce and the meat stock. Put into a low oven until most of the liquid has been absorbed but the food is not dry—about ½ hour.

25 tortillas
1 cup oil or lard
1 pound Mexican green tomatoes, quartered
4 *serrano* chiles
1 medium onion, roughly chopped
1 clove garlic, chopped
2 *epazote* leaves (if available)
3 sprigs coriander, or ¼ teaspoon ground
1 teaspoon salt
1½ cups grated cheese
1 cup beef stock

Mix the dry ingredients together in a bowl, then work in the lard, adding enough water to hold the dough together. Divide the dough into twelve equal balls. Flatten these either on a tortilla press or between pieces of waxed paper with a rolling pin into tortillas of about ⅛ inch thick. Place 2 tablespoons of the following filling in the center of the tortilla.

Sauté the onion in butter until soft; add the tomatoes and cook for 3 minutes. Combine all the filling ingredients.

Fold over the filled tortilla as for a turnover and pinch the edges to seal them. Place on a greased baking sheet and let them rest for 10 minutes. Bake in a preheated moderate oven for 10 to 15 minutes. Serve immediately with the following sauce on the side.

Sauté the onions and garlic in olive oil until they begin to brown. Add all the other ingredients except the olives and cook for 10 minutes. Add the olives just before serving.

A variation for the filling would be ½ pound cooked crabmeat instead of the sardines.

3 cups sifted flour
2 teaspoons baking powder
1 teaspoon salt
¾ cup lard
Approximately ½ cup water

Filling:
1 onion, finely chopped
1 tablespoon butter
2 tomatoes, peeled and chopped
2 hard-boiled eggs, chopped
2 cans boneless sardines
3 tablespoons chopped, pitted olives
⅛ teaspoon cayenne pepper
¼ teaspoon oregano

Sauce:
2 onions, chopped
3 cloves garlic, finely chopped
⅓ cup olive oil
4 tomatoes, peeled and chopped
2 canned pimientos, chopped
2 tablespoons capers
¼ cup medium sherry
Salt and pepper to taste
½ cup sliced olives

ENCHILADAS DE MOLE

(These enchiladas may be made with *mole* left over from *Mole de Guajolote* or with cubed or powdered *mole* available in special shops. If you use the cubes or the powder, add a small quantity of chicken stock and a square of cooking chocolate after you have fried the powder with a little pork fat, then add all of it in the blender with some fried prunes, raisins, almonds, and a little powdered sugar and salt. This will make a thick sauce, which should be allowed to simmer for 10 minutes.)

Dip the tortillas in hot oil just until soft. Remove and lay on absorbent paper. Fill with the cooked, shredded chicken or turkey breast and roll them into tubes. Lay them seam side down on a shallow baking dish and cover with *mole* sauce. Bake in a moderate (300°) oven for 15 minutes. Just before serving, sprinkle the sesame seeds over the top.

12 tortillas
⅓ cup corn oil
4 chicken breasts or same quantity of turkey breast
1½ cups *Mole* Sauce
2 tablespoons toasted sesame seeds

ENCHILADAS ESTILO JALISCO

Fry the tomatoes and onion with 2 of the green peppers in 1 tablespoon of the oil until soft. Add the sour cream, salt, and rum. Simmer a few minutes to blend the flavors. For the filling, mix the remaining 2 chopped peppers, radishes, the avocados, and the cream cheese. Fry the tortillas in hot oil just until soft. Then dip them in the sauce and fill each with 2 tablespoons of the chopped vegetables and cheese. Roll these filled tortillas and lay them seam side down in a shallow baking dish. Pour the sauce over all and bake for 15 minutes in a moderate oven.

2 medium tomatoes, peeled and chopped
1 onion, chopped
4 green peppers, seeded and chopped
¼ cup corn oil
½ cup sour cream
Salt to taste
1 tablespoon rum
10 radishes, chopped
2 avocados, diced
12 ounces cream cheese
12 tortillas

GORDITAS

Mix the *masa*, lard, salt, and enough water to make a smooth dough. Divide into 12 parts; roll each part into a ball. Pat between the palms of your hands, singing "Angelitos Negros," into small pancakes of about ¼ inch thick. Pinch each cake around the edges to form a slightly raised border. Deep-fry in hot oil until golden brown and drain on absorbent paper. Fill the *gorditas* with *Frijoles Refritos* and top with grated cheese.
Makes 12 *gorditas*.

2 cups *masa harina*
2 tablespoons lard
1 teaspoon salt
Approximately 1 cup water
Corn oil

PAPATZUL

Remove the casings from the sausages and fry in 1 tablespoon of the lard for a few minutes. Drain on paper towels and mix the crumbled sausage meat with the chopped eggs. Puree the onion and garlic with ½ teaspoon *epazote* in a blender. Sauté this puree in remaining 2 tablespoons hot lard for 5 minutes, stirring, then add tomatoes and season to taste. Cook the sauce for 5 more minutes and set aside. Grind the pumpkin seeds in a blender, adding the chiles and remaining ½ teaspoon *epazote*. Put this mixture in a pot and gradually add the chicken stock, stirring constantly. Simmer slowly until the sauce is thick. Do not allow to boil. Dip the tortillas in the pumpkin-seed sauce and coat each well on both sides. Lay the dipped tortilla on a dish, fill it with chopped egg and *chorizo*, then roll it into a tube and lay it, seam side down, in a shallow baking dish. Pour all the remaining pumpkin sauce over the rolled tortillas and top with the tomato sauce. Bake in a preheated low oven for 15 minutes.

2 *chorizo* sausages
3 tablespoons lard
6 hard-boiled eggs, chopped
1 onion, roughly chopped
2 cloves garlic, finely chopped
1 teaspoon crumbled *epazote* leaves
4 tomatoes, peeled, seeded, and chopped
Salt and pepper to taste
1½ cups pumpkin seeds
4 *serrano* chiles
2 cups chicken stock
12 tortillas

QUESADILLAS CON TUÉTANO

Bake the marrow bones in a preheated low oven for 20 minutes. Scrape the marrow out and chop it. Mix together the *masa*, flour, salt, and baking soda, finally adding enough water to make a smooth dough. Shape into 12 balls by patting between hands while singing the Mexican national anthem until you have made slightly thick tortillas, about ⅛ inch, about 3 inches across. Place a generous slice of cooking cheese with 1 teaspoon chopped onion in the center of each tortilla, fold in half, and pinch the edges to seal. Fry in deep hot oil until golden brown. Drain on paper towels and serve immediately with your favorite hot sauce.

1 pound beef marrow bones
2 cups *masa harina*
¼ cup sifted flour
1 teaspoon salt
½ teaspoon baking soda
Approximately 1 to 1½ cups water
1 copy, sheet music, of Mexico's anthem
12 slabs of cooking cheese
2 medium onions, finely chopped
Corn oil

TACOS DE MOCHAMOS

Cook the pork in 1½ cups salted water until the water has evaporated—approximately 30 minutes, depending on altitude. Allow to cool, then shred the pork. Fry the shredded meat in the lard until golden brown. Dip the tortillas in hot oil just until soft, remove to absorbent paper, fill with the meat, and roll into tubes. Fasten with toothpicks. If you desire crisp tortillas: when the go-go tortillas have been filled and rolled and pinned, refry them in the hot oil until golden brown. Serve with Guacamole or *Salsa Mexicana*.

1 pound pork
1 teaspoon salt
1 to 2 teaspoons lard
12 tortillas
⅓ cup corn oil (for soft tacos), or
    1 cup corn oil (for hard tacos)

TACOS DE POLLO

Dip the tortillas in hot oil just until soft, remove to absorbent paper, fill with the shredded chicken breasts, and roll into a tube, pinned closed with toothpicks. If you want crisp tortillas, refry them in the hot oil until golden brown. Serve with Guacamole.

12 tortillas
⅓ cup corn oil (for soft tacos), or
    1 cup corn oil (for hard tacos)
4 cooked chicken breasts

TORTAS DE JAMÓN Y QUESO

Split the *bolillos* and fry the soft sides in hot lard (using only a little at a time). Spread warm refried beans on the bottom half of the sandwich. Top this with cheese, ham, *jalapeño* halves, and shredded lettuce. Cover with top half of sandwich.

4 *bolillos* (chunky slices of French bread)
¼ cup lard
½ cup Refried Beans
4 slices Monterey Jack cheese
4 slices cooked ham
4 *jalapeño* chiles, halved and seeded
Shredded lettuce

TOSTADAS DE FRIJOL

Fry the tortillas in hot oil until lightly browned and stiff. Drain on paper towels and sprinkle with salt. Keep warm in a low oven. Spread the tortillas with refried beans and sprinkle generously with cheese. Put in oven or under broiler until cheese just begins to melt. Serve with *Salsa Verde*.

12 fresh or canned tortillas
½ cup corn oil
1½ cups Refried Beans
2 cups grated Cheddar cheese

TOSTADAS DE POLLO

Fry the tortillas in hot oil until lightly browned and stiff. Drain on paper towels and sprinkle with salt. Keep warm in a low oven. Spread the tortillas with refried beans. Top with shredded chicken, lettuce, and tomato. Sprinkle some grated cheese over it. Mix the two creams together and dribble 1½ table-spoons over each *tostada*. Serve with Guacamole or your favorite hot sauce, or put slices of *jalapeños* on all of it.

12 fresh or canned tortillas
½ cup corn oil
Salt to taste
1½ cups Refried Beans
2 chicken breasts, cooked and shredded
1 small head Boston lettuce
4 tomatoes, chopped
½ cup grated Parmesan cheese
½ cup sour cream
½ cup fresh heavy cream

TOSTADAS TAPATÍAS

Fry the tortillas in hot oil until lightly browned. Drain on paper towels and sprinkle with salt. Keep warm in low oven. Spread the tortillas with refried beans. Top with grated cheese, chopped sausage, radishes, and lettuce. Serve immediately with Guacamole or your favorite hot sauce.

12 fresh or canned tortillas
½ cup corn oil
Salt to taste
1½ cups Refried Beans
½ cup grated cheese
3 *chorizo* sausages, skinned, chopped, and fried
10 radishes, sliced
1 small head Boston lettuce, shredded

TOSTADITAS

With scissors cut the tortillas into quarters and fry in hot oil until brown. Drain on absorbent paper and salt while hot. These may be prepared in advance and are served to garnish or to be used for dips such as Guacamole or Pureed Beans.

Tortillas
Corn oil
Salt to taste

TOTOPOS

Prepare the chiles as indicated in Part II, Stage One, but grind them in a blender with ¾ cup of the liquid in which they soaked.

Mash the cooked beans. Mix together the chiles, beans, *masa,* and salt, then add enough water to make a smooth dough. Divide the dough into 12 equal parts and pat each between the palms of your hands into a 2½-inch pancake. Cook these on a dry *comal* or heavy iron skillet. Before serving, fry them in hot oil until golden brown. Remove to absorbent paper and top with Guacamole.
Makes 12 *totopos.*

2 *ancho* chiles
½ cup cooked red or black beans
2 cups *masa harina*
1 teaspoon salt
2 tablespoons lard
Approximately ½ cup water
Corn oil

TAMALES DE POLLO AL ESTILO DE SEÑORA KEIFETZ

Remove any silk which might be on the corn shucks. Soak the shucks in cold water until ready to use. Any that were torn in half may be used to steam the tamales. Boil the chicken for 20 minutes in water with salt and 1 clove garlic. Remove the chicken and let it cool, reserving the broth. Chop the chicken into medium-size pieces. Put the pieces into the *salsa verde* in a saucepan, add chopped green chiles, and simmer for 10 minutes. Add the chopped chicken, 2 cloves garlic, finely chopped, the cumin, and ½ cup chicken stock, and cook 5 more minutes.

In a shallow bowl make the tamale dough: Mix the baking powder and 1 teaspoon salt with the *masa* flour, then gradually blending in the lard with your fingers and adding sufficient chicken stock to make a soft, semidry dough that will not stick to your hands when you press your palm down on it. Spread the *masa* on the corn shucks in this manner: Lay a corn shuck in the palm of your hand with the narrow end toward your fingertips. Spread the *masa* over the bottom half of the shucks only, applying pressure with the back of a tablespoon. Turn the shucks to do the sides if you wish. When all the shucks are prepared, fill with 2 tablespoons of the chicken mixture each and fold. Fold the left side over, then the right (which should overlap the seam

Corn shucks
8 chicken breasts
Salt
3 cloves garlic
Chicken stock
21 ounces *Salsa Verde* (or 3 cans Herdez Salsa Verde)
1 4-ounce can green chiles, chopped
1 teaspoon ground cumin
½ teaspoon baking powder
1 pound *masa harina*
½ pound lard

a little), then fold the narrow, unfilled, end down, thus leaving one end open.

Put 5 cups chicken stock in a large pot with a rack. Cover the rack with filled corn shucks and stand the tamales, open end up, on this. Cover the tamales with more corn shucks, then a damp cloth, and cover tightly. Steam over medium heat until the *masa* no longer clings to the shuck—about 2 hours. (Makes 30 tamales.)

FISH *MARISCOS Y PESCADOS*

AVOCADO STUFFED WITH SHRIMP
Aguacates Rellenos con Camarones

SHRIMP RICE
Arroz con Camarones

MARINATED FISH COCKTAIL
Ceviche Estilo Rey de los Reyes

VERA CRUZ RED SNAPPER
Huachinango a la Veracruzana

VERA CRUZ CRAB
Jaiba Verucruzana

OYSTER STEW
Ostiones Guisados

FISH IN HAZELNUT SAUCE
Pescado en Salsa de Avellanas

DRUNKEN FISH
Pescado Borracho

SHRIMP IN GREEN PUMPKIN SAUCE
Pipián Verde de Camarones

FISH WITH PARSLEY
Pescado con Perejil

FISH IN ALMOND AND WALNUT SAUCE
Pescado en Salsa de Almendra y Nuez

AVOCADO STUFFED WITH SHRIMP

Aguacates Rellenos con Camarones

Halve the avocados, discard the pits, and scoop out all the fruit, saving the shell. Mash the avocados in a bowl, then mix in the shrimp (to my preference, cut in half), eggs, olives, *jalapeño*, onion, and *cilantro*. Add the mayonnaise and salt and pepper to taste. Blend thoroughly. Serve with tortilla chips and lemon or lime wedges.
Serves 6.

3 large avocados
1 pound shrimp, cooked and cleaned
2 hard-boiled eggs, chopped
24 green olives, pitted and finely chopped
1 *jalapeño* chile, seeded and finely chopped (or more if you wish)
1 tablespoon grated onion
1 tablespoon chopped *cilantro*
½ cup mayonnaise
Salt and pepper to taste

SHRIMP RICE

Arroz con Camarones

Put the tomato, onion, and garlic into a blender and puree. Fry the rice in oil until golden. Add the puree and fry for 2 minutes, stirring. Transfer the tomato-rice mixture to a pot with a lid; add salt, pepper, shrimp, and 2 cups water. Cook over low heat until all the liquid has been absorbed—about 30 minutes.
Serves 4.

1 large tomato, peeled, seeded, and quartered
½ small onion, cut up
1 clove garlic, sliced
1 cup short-grain rice
3 tablespoons corn oil
Salt and pepper to taste
1½ pounds peeled, raw shrimp
2 cups water

MARINATED FISH COCKTAIL

Ceviche Estilo Rey de los Reyes

Marinate the fish in the juice for 6 hours in the refrigerator, giving it a stir once or twice. Add all the remaining ingredients except avocado and keep chilled until ready to serve. Just before serving, add diced avocado.

Serves 6.

1 pound mackerel, boned and cut into ½-inch pieces (red snapper, crabmeat, octopus, and abalone can also be used)

Juice of 6 limes or lemons

2 tomatoes, peeled, seeded, and chopped

1 onion, finely chopped

3 fresh green chiles (such as *serranos*), seeded and finely chopped

3 tablespoons olive oil

¼ tablespoon oregano

1 tablespoon parsley, finely chopped

1 small avocado, peeled, diced (optional)

VERA CRUZ RED SNAPPER

Huachinango a la Veracruzana

Bathe fish in juice for ½ hour. Meanwhile, sauté the onions, garlic, and pimientos in olive oil until soft—about 5 minutes. Add the tomato puree and remaining ingredients and cook for 20 minutes over low heat. Place the fish in a large casserole and pour the sauce over all. Bake in preheated moderate oven for 25 minutes. A suggested accompaniment is *Torta de Papas al Limón.*
Serves 6.

3 pounds red snapper (or other ocean fish) fillets
5 tablespoons lime or lemon juice
2 onions, chopped
2 cloves garlic, finely chopped
2 pimientos, sliced
3 tablespoons olive oil
2 cups tomato puree
3 *jalapeño* chiles, seeded and thinly sliced
15 green olives, pitted, sliced
2 tablespoons capers
¼ cup dry sherry
4 tablespoons vinegar
½ tablespoon oregano
⅛ teaspoon ground cinnamon
⅛ teaspoon ground cloves
3 sprigs parsley, chopped
Salt and pepper to taste

VERA CRUZ CRAB

Jaiba Veracruzana

Sauté the onion and garlic in olive oil until soft. Add the tomato puree and spices. When this begins to simmer, add the crab, olives, capers, chile, pimientos, and salt. Cook for 5 minutes, then stir in the cream. Beat the yolks and whites of the eggs separately until frothy, then fold together. Transfer the crab mixture into a greased baking dish and top with the whipped eggs. Sprinkle grated cheese over all and bake in a moderate oven for 15 minutes. Possible companion: *Camote con Fruta.*
Serves 6.

1 large onion, chopped
3 cloves garlic, finely chopped
4 tablespoons olive oil
1¼ cups tomato puree
⅛ teaspoon ground cloves
⅛ teaspoon cinnamon
1½ pounds lump crabmeat
15 stuffed olives, sliced
1 tablespoon capers
1 *jalapeño* chile, finely chopped with seeds
2 pimientos, sliced in thin strips
Salt to taste
⅓ cup light cream
3 eggs, separated
¼ cup grated cheese

OYSTER STEW

Ostiones Guisados

Drain the oysters and reserve the liquid. Sauté the green pepper, onions, garlic, and parsley in olive oil until soft. Add the tomato puree and cook until simmering. Add the reserved oyster juice, spices, and olives, stirring well to blend. Add the potatoes, cover, and cook until the potatoes are done. Pour in the oysters and the vinegar and cook over low heat or until the oysters are done—about 10 minutes. *Do not overcook.*
Serves 6.

1½ pints oysters
½ green pepper, seeded and chopped
2 onions, chopped
2 cloves garlic, finely chopped
1 teaspoon chopped parsley
2 tablespoons olive oil
2 cups tomato puree
¼ teaspoon oregano
⅛ teaspoon cayenne pepper
⅛ teaspoon ground cinnamon
1 teaspoon salt
Pinch of ground cloves
12 green olives, pitted and chopped
3 potatoes, peeled and cubed
1 tablespoon vinegar

FISH IN HAZELNUT SAUCE

Pescado en Salsa de Avellanas

Cook the fillets in white wine with the onion, bay leaf, thyme, marjoram, parsley, salt, and pepper, covered, until they flake easily with a fork—about 10 minutes. Remove gently to shallow casserole and keep warm in very low oven. Fry bread in hot oil. Take skillet from heat, reserving it for a moment. Grind the hazelnuts, bread, parsley, garlic, and saffron as finely as possible in the blender. Strain the white wine stock. Stir the ground nuts into the hot oil and add the stock. Cook for 10 minutes, stirring occasionally. Pour the sauce over the fish and serve. Serves 6.

6 fish fillets
2 cups dry white wine
1 onion cut in half
1 bay leaf
⅛ teaspoon thyme
⅛ teaspoon marjoram
2 sprigs parsley
1 teaspoon salt
½ teaspoon coarsely ground pepper
1 slice bread
3 tablespoons olive oil
¾ cup hazelnuts, roasted for 10 minutes in 400°
    oven and peeled
1 tablespoon chopped parsley
1 clove garlic
Pinch of saffron
Salt and pepper to taste

DRUNKEN FISH

Pescado Borracho

Prepare the chiles as in Part II, Stage One. Coat the fish in flour seasoned with salt and pepper. Brown the fish in hot oil lightly on both sides. Gently remove to a large casserole with a lid. In the same oil sauté the onion and garlic until soft. Add the chile puree, tomatoes, cumin, oregano, salt, and pepper. Simmer, stirring, for 5 minutes. Mix in the olives, sugar, and red wine. Pour this sauce over the fish and bake, covered, in a preheated moderate oven until the fish flakes easily with a fork—about ½ hour.

Company for the drunk: Mexican Rice and *Habas con Queso.*
Serves 6.

6 *ancho* chiles
1 5-pound whole white ocean fish
Flour
Salt and pepper to taste
¼ cup olive oil
1 onion, finely chopped
2 cloves garlic, finely chopped
3 large tomatoes, peeled, seeded, and chopped
¼ teaspoon ground cumin
1 teaspoon oregano
1 cup pimiento-stuffed olives, cut into thirds
1 teaspoon sugar
2 cups dry red wine

SHRIMP IN GREEN PUMPKIN SAUCE

Pipián Verde de Camarones

Cook the shrimp in boiling water, covered, for 5 minutes. When cool, peel. Finely grind the *pepitas* in the blender. Remove and set aside. Puree the onion, garlic, coriander, green tomatoes, and *jalapeños* in the blender. Mix this puree with the *pepitas*, salt, and crushed coriander seeds. Sauté this sauce in olive oil for 5 minutes, stirring. Add the chicken broth and simmer another minute. Add the shrimp and heat; do not allow to boil. At the last minute, add the lemon juice.

2 pounds raw shrimp
1 cup pumpkin seeds (*pepitas*)
1 small onion, chopped
2 cloves garlic, finely chopped
4 sprigs fresh coriander (*cilantro*), or ⅛ teaspoon ground coriander
1 10-ounce can Mexican green tomatoes, drained
2 *jalapeño* chiles
1 teaspoon salt
1 teaspoon broken or crushed coriander seeds
3 tablespoons olive oil
1 cup chicken broth
1 tablespoon lemon juice

FISH WITH PARSLEY

Pescado con Perejil

Drain the green tomatoes and reserve the liquid. Grind the tomatoes in the blender. Combine the onion, garlic, parsley, *cilantro*, cumin, salt, and pepper with the tomatoes. In a buttered baking dish spread half the sauce. Lay the fish fillets over this and spread the remaining sauce over the fish. Sprinkle with lemon juice and bake in a moderate oven until the fish flakes easily with a fork—about 20 minutes. Should the fish seem dry, moisten with a little of the green tomato sauce. Suggested accompaniment: *Coliflor Estilo Puebla.*
Serves 6.

1 10-ounce can Mexican green tomatoes
1 onion, finely chopped (½ cup)
2 cloves garlic, finely chopped
1 cup finely chopped parsley
1 tablespoon *cilantro*
¼ teaspoon ground cumin
Salt and pepper to taste
6 fillets red fish, or flounder, or similar fish
Juice 1 lemon

FISH IN ALMOND AND WALNUT SAUCE

Pescado en Salsa de Almendra y Nuez

Cook the fish with the onions and garlic in the white wine and the liquid from the can of tomatoes (1 cup). Add salt and pepper. The fish should simmer, covered, until it flakes easily with a fork—about 15 minutes.

Gently remove the cooked fish to a shallow baking dish and keep warm in a very low oven; reserve liquid.

Put the almonds, walnuts, chiles, coriander, and the liquid in which the fish cooked, including the onions and the garlic, in a blender. This may be done all at once or in two lots depending on the size of the blender. Blend until smooth. Heat sauce without allowing it to boil. Pour over the fish and serve immediately.

Suggested accompaniment: Crown of Rice or *Arroz Tabasqueño.*

Serves 6.

3 pounds white lean fish fillets such as flounder or red fish
2 onions, chopped
1 clove garlic, finely chopped
1 cup dry white wine
1 10-ounce can Mexican green tomatoes
Salt and pepper to taste
½ cup blanched almonds
½ cup walnuts
3 canned *jalapeño* chiles
4 sprigs coriander (*cilantro*), or ⅛ teaspoon ground coriander

POULTRY *AVES DE CORRAL*

CHICKEN CREPES
Crepes de Pollo en Salsa Verde

CHICKENS IN OVERCOATS
Pollos en Abrigos

CHICKEN IN PINE-NUT SAUCE
Pollo con Salsa de Piñones

CHICKEN TABASCO
Pollo Tabasqueño

CINDERELLA IN PUMPKIN
Pipián de Pepitas a la Cenicienta

DRUNKEN POULES DE LUXE
Pollitos Borrachos

FRIED CHICKEN TO THE TASTE OF COLONEL FERDINAND FAIRFAX
Pollo Frito al Gusto del Coronel Fernando Fairfax

QUAIL IN CASSEROLE
Cordornices en Cazuela

TABLECLOTH STAINER
Mancha Manteles

TURKEY MOLE
Mole de Guajolote

SUPREMELY STUFFED DUCK
Pato Relleno Supremo

CHICKEN CREPES

Crepas de Pollo en Salsa Verde

Combine eggs, milk, butter, and salt. Add to the sifted flour and beat until smooth. Pour 3 tablespoons of batter on a 7-inch greased skillet. Tilt the pan until the batter has spread evenly over the bottom. When lightly browned, turn the crepe and brown the other side. Stack until all crepes are made.

Sauté the onion in butter until soft. Add the tomatoes and simmer for 5 minutes. Add remaining ingredients and simmer for 5 more minutes. Take pan off the heat. Put a tablespoon of filling in each crepe, roll into a tube, and lay in a buttered glass baking dish. Pour green sauce over the crepes.

Lay the green peppers under the broiler and singe them on all sides. Wrap them in a damp towel for ½ hour. Then peel the skin off, remove stems and seeds, and grind in a blender or chop very finely. Sauté pepper and onion in butter for 5 minutes. Dissolve the cornstarch in the milk; add to the pepper-and-onion mixture; simmer gently for 3 minutes. Add ¼ cup of the grated cheese and stir until the cheese is melted and well blended. Pour the sauce over the crepes and shake remaining cheese over the top. Bake in moderate oven for 10 minutes. Makes 10–12 crepes.

Crepe Batter:
2 eggs, well beaten
⅔ cup milk
1 tablespoon melted butter
½ tablespoon salt
½ cup sifted, all-purpose flour

Crepe Filling:
1 medium onion, finely chopped
2 tablespoons butter
2 medium tomatoes, peeled and chopped
2 large chicken breasts, cooked and diced
¼ cup almonds, blanched and slivered
1 tablespoon chopped raisins
1 tablespoon capers
8 stuffed olives, chopped
2 small *jalapeño* chiles, finely chopped

Green Sauce:
4 small green peppers
2 tablespoons finely chopped onion
2 tablespoons butter
1½ tablespoons cornstarch
1½ cups milk
½ cup grated Swiss cheese

CHICKENS IN OVERCOATS

Pollos en Abrigos

Fry chicken in oil until browned on all sides. In a deep casserole with a lid, place a layer of chicken covered with a layer of fruits and vegetables. Drip oil sparingly over all and sprinkle with salt and pepper. Make another layer of chicken and cover with remaining fruits and vegetables. Drip oil over all and sprinkle with salt and pepper. Cover the casserole and place in a moderate oven for 2½ hours. Serve with Mexican Rice. Serves 6.

1 large chicken, cut in serving pieces, or
    6 chicken portions of your choice
½ cup corn oil
3 tablespoons olive oil
1 large onion, thinly sliced
3 large tomatoes, peeled and sliced
1 pound zucchini, thinly sliced
2 pears, peeled, cored, and sliced
2 bananas, sliced
1 cup pineapple chunks
Salt and pepper to taste

CHICKEN IN PINE-NUT SAUCE

Pollo con Salsa de Piñones

Stew the chicken pieces in 2 quarts water seasoned with onion, salt, pepper, and carrot until tender—about 45 minutes for a young chicken. Grind or finely chop the dry, blanched pine nuts and brown lightly in oil. Add sherry, cinnamon, sugar, and flour. Cook for 5 minutes, stirring constantly. Add the chicken pieces and the strained stock and cook for another 15 minutes. Add the raisins and the almond halves and simmer 10 more minutes. For company: String Beans with Green Peppers and/or Green Rice. Serves 4.

1 chicken, cut in quarters, or your favorite
    chicken portions
1 onion
Salt and pepper to taste
1 carrot
½ cup blanched pine nuts
¼ cup corn oil
½ cup sherry
1 tablespoon ground cinnamon
2 tablespoons sugar
2 tablespoons flour
¼ cup seedless raisins
¼ cup blanched almond halves

CHICKEN TABASCO

Pollo Tabasqueño

Rub the chicken with lime juice (Rose's unsweetened lime juice may be used) and sprinkle with salt. Fry in hot oil to a golden brown. Pour off excess oil, leaving 3 or 4 tablespoons. Remove chicken and set aside in a flameproof casserole with a lid. In the same skillet sauté all the remaining ingredients for 10 minutes. Pour the sauce over the chicken, add 1½ cups water, and simmer, covered, for 1¼ hours.

Company: Rice Tabasqueño.

Serves 6.

1 5-pound chicken, cut into serving pieces
3 tablespoons lime juice
Salt
⅓ cup corn oil
3 medium onions, finely chopped
6 medium tomatoes, peeled and chopped
5 stuffed olives, chopped
2 tablespoons seedless raisins
3 pitted prunes, chopped
¼ pound ham, finely chopped
⅓ cup chopped blanched almonds
8 cloves garlic, finely chopped
2 tablespoons wine vinegar
2 tablespoons olive oil
1 stick cinnamon
4 cloves

CINDERELLA IN PUMPKIN

Pipián de Pepitas a la Cenicienta

Prepare the chiles as described in Part II, Stage One. Boil the chicken pieces in 3 cups salted water until tender. Drain and reserve 2 cups stock. Grind the *pepitas* in a blender as fine as possible and set aside. Put the prepared chiles, garlic, onion, *epazote,* and tomatoes in a blender and grind to a coarse puree, a little at a time. Heat the lard in a skillet and fry the puree with the ground pumpkin seeds and toasted sesame seeds for 5 minutes, stirring. Add salt and pepper to taste and the chicken stock. The sauce should have the consistency of heavy cream. Add the chicken pieces and simmer slowly for 15 minutes. For company: Zucchini and cream and white rice.
Serves 4.

6 *ancho* chiles
1 chicken, cut into serving pieces
2 cups chicken stock
1 cup *pepitas* (pumpkin seeds), husks removed
3 cloves garlic
1 large onion, chopped
1 sprig *epazote,* if available
6 medium tomatoes, peeled, seeded, and
    chopped
2 tablespoons lard
¼ cup toasted sesame seeds
Salt and pepper to taste

DRUNKEN POULES DE LUXE

Pollitos Borrachos

Use a large paella dish or a large flameproof casserole. Fry the chicken in hot oil until golden brown. Add the tomatoes and onion and fry for 10 more minutes, stirring occasionally. Add the remaining ingredients and mix everything together. Cover and simmer 20 minutes. For company: *Corona de Frijol* and white rice.
Serves 8.

2 small chickens, quartered
½ cup corn oil
2 large tomatoes, peeled and chopped
1 medium onion, chopped
½ pound ham, chopped
2 cups sherry
¼ cup sugar
¼ teaspoon cinnamon
¼ teaspoon ground cloves
⅛ teaspoon nutmeg
⅓ cup seedless raisins
¼ cup chopped blanched almonds

FRIED CHICKEN TO THE TASTE OF COLONEL FERDINAND FAIRFAX

Pollo Frito al Gusto del Coronel Fernando Fairfax

Boil the chicken in the water with carrot, onion, celery, garlic clove, and 1 teaspoon salt for ½ hour, covered. Remove chicken and set aside. Strain the stock and reserve the liquid. Pour the chicken stock into a pot with the tomatoes, chopped onion, 2 cloves garlic, seasonings, and honey. Simmer until thick. Fry the cooked chicken in combined corn and olive oil to a golden brown. Drain on paper towels. Serve with the sauce poured over. For company: *Frijoles Rancheros.*
Serves 8.

2 chickens, cut into quarters
2½ cups water
1 carrot
1 onion
1 stalk celery
1 clove garlic
1 teaspoon salt
4 tomatoes, peeled, seeded, and chopped
1 large onion, finely chopped
2 cloves garlic
¼ teaspoon cinnamon
⅛ teaspoon nutmeg
¼ teaspoon thyme
1 teaspoon oregano
Salt and pepper to taste
1 tablespoon honey
½ cup corn oil
3 tablespoons olive oil

QUAIL IN CASSEROLE

Cordornices en Cazuela

Brown the quail in lard, remove, and set aside. In the same fat, sauté the onions, garlic, parsley, and tomatoes for 5 minutes. Add the cloves, cumin, and bread crumbs, stirring well. Add the broth, salt, vinegar, oregano, and capers. Place the quail in a casserole, cover with the sauce, and cook over low heat for 2 hours. Just before serving, add the olive oil, chiles, and olives. Dove may be used in place of quail. For company: White rice and *Calabacitas del Sur.*

Serves 6.

12 quail
6 tablespoons lard
3 onions, finely chopped
3 cloves garlic, finely chopped
9 sprigs parsley
12 tomatoes, peeled, seeded, and pureed
¼ teaspoon ground cloves
½ teaspoon ground cumin
9 slices French bread, crumbled
2½ cups chicken broth
½ teaspoon salt
1½ tablespoons vinegar
1½ teaspoons oregano
2 tablespoons capers
3 tablespoons olive oil
6 green chiles, chopped
4 tablespoons sliced olives

TABLECLOTH STAINER

Mancha Manteles

Fry the chicken in oil until brown. Remove. Pour off excess oil. Melt the lard in the skillet. Remove veins from chiles and tear into pieces. Fry the chile pieces lightly in lard with almonds and sesame seeds. Remove and grind in blender while mixture is still hot. Fry the *chorizo* sausage in remaining lard for 3 minutes and lift out. In the same fat sauté sliced onion until soft and add the chiles, almonds, sesame seeds, tomatoes, and cinnamon. Simmer this mixture a few minutes stirring occasionally. Transfer the sauce to a good-size casserole with a lid. Stir in the stock, add the browned chicken, sliced fruits, sausage bits, chiles, sugar, vinegar, and salt. Cover and simmer for 1 hour. For company: Spiced rice.
Serves 8.

2 small frying chickens, quartered
½ cup corn oil
2 tablespoons lard
2 *ancho* chiles
2 *pasilla* chiles
3 *jalapeño* chiles, chopped
½ cup chopped blanched almonds
3 teaspoons sesame seeds
2 *chorizo* sausages, peeled and chopped
1 onion, thinly sliced
½ pound tomatoes, peeled, seeded, and chopped
1 teaspoon cinnamon
2 cups chicken stock
2 slices fresh or canned pineapple, cut into chunks
2 apples, peeled, cored, and sliced
1 large green banana, peeled and sliced
1 tablespoon sugar
1½ tablespoons vinegar
1 teaspoon salt

TURKEY MOLE

Mole de Guajolote

The oldest surviving evolved recipe of cooked food of any system of cooking of any of the ancient civilizations of the world.

As the Mayas ate it 9000 years ago, as the Emperor Moctezuma served it to Hernán Cortés:

Put the pieces of turkey into a large pot with onion, celery, and salt. Add water to cover and boil until tender—about 2½ hours. Clean the chiles, reserving some of the seeds for desired piquancy. Boil the *chipotle* chiles until tender and puree in blender with the tomatoes. All chiles must be veined and seeded. Tear the *mulato, ancho,* and *pasilla* chiles into pieces and fry them lightly in 2 tablespoons of the lard. Lift them out and reserve. Toast the sesame seeds in the oven until lightly browned. In the same skillet with the used lard, fry the almonds, the peanuts, raisins, tortilla torn into pieces, cloves, cinnamon, and peppercorns. Grind the following in the blender: the reserved chile seeds, fried ingredients, onion, and garlic. You will have to do this in two or three lots. To facilitate the grinding, add ½ cup turkey stock to each lot in the blender. (By now the turkey will have been cooking close to an hour.) Dissolve this mixture and the chocolate in 1 pint

1 8-pound turkey, cut into serving pieces
1 onion
1 stalk celery
Salt to taste
2 *chipotle* chiles
6 *mulato* chiles
6 *ancho* chiles
4 *pasilla* chiles
4 tablespoons lard
3 tablespoons sesame seeds
⅓ cup almonds
⅓ cup peanuts
¼ cup raisins
1 tortilla
¼ teaspoon ground cloves
¼ teaspoon cinnamon
4 peppercorns
1 teaspoon (or more) seeds reserved from chiles
1 large onion, roughly chopped
3 cloves garlic, chopped
1 quart turkey stock
1 ounce unsweetened chocolate
3 medium tomatoes, peeled

stock. Fry the tomatoes and *chipotle* puree in remaining 2 tablespoons lard for 10 minutes, stirring occasionally. Add 1 cup stock and simmer for 10 more minutes. Add this to the *mole,* along with any remaining stock, and simmer, stirring occasionally, for 1 hour. Serve over the turkey, which has been skinned and boned, with white or sesame rice and Puree Beans.

Use the leftover turkey stock for Zucchini and Turkey Soup.

SUPREMELY STUFFED DUCK

Pato Relleno Supremo

Wash and dry the duck. Rub it inside and out with cut orange and sprinkle with salt and pepper. Let it sit for 15 minutes while you mix the ground pork and ham with the sliced olives, raisins, ½ teaspoon salt, ½ teaspoon pepper, 4 sprigs parsley, chopped eggs, raw egg, and ¼ cup of the sherry. Stuff the duck with this mixture and fasten the opening in the duck.

Sauté the duck in lard and oil until browned. Add the garlic, onions, and 1 tablespoon chopped parsley to the fat and sauté for 5 more minutes. Add 1½ cups water and the remaining ¼ cup sherry. Cover tightly and simmer over low heat for 3 hours. Remove duck to a platter and keep warm. Skim the fat off the top of the gravy—it is impossible to get all of it. Add the ground almonds and cook, stirring, until it thickens—about 10 minutes. Serve sauce in a gravy boat, with the duck.

Serves 4.

1 large duck
1 sour orange
Salt and pepper to taste
½ pound ground pork loin
¼ pound ground ham
3 tablespoons sliced pitted olives
2 tablespoons raisins
½ teaspoon salt
½ teaspoon ground pepper
4 sprigs parsley, chopped
2 hard-boiled eggs, chopped
1 raw egg
½ cup dry sherry
4 tablespoons lard
2 tablespoons olive oil
2 cloves garlic, finely chopped
3 onions, chopped
1 tablespoon chopped parsley
2 ounces ground almonds

MEATS *CARNES*

BEEFSTEAK FOR DESMOND GUINNESS
Biftec con Cerveza

BEEF MAZATLÁN
Carne de Res de Mazatlán

RUM HASH
Picadillo con Ron

TAMPICO STEAKS
Carne Asada a la Tampiqueña

RED-HOT BEEFSTEAK AND MUSHROOMS
Biftec con Chipotles y Hongos

MEAT LOAF IN HAZELNUT SAUCE
Lomo en Salsa de Avellanas

MEATBALLS ABOUNDING
Albóndigas

BEEF STEW
Estofado de Res

UPHOLSTERED LEG OF LAMB
Pierna de Carnero Estofado

TWELVE-FLAVORED LAMB
Adobo de Carnero

PORK MOLE
Mole de Chile Serrano

AZTEC PORK PIE TO THE TASTE OF BIANCA JAGGER
Torta Azteca al Gusto de Bianca Jagger

EIGHT-FLAVORED PORK
Lomo de Puerco Adobo

YSABEL DEIGHTON'S PIGLET
Carnitas de Puerco de Ysabel Deighton

VEAL IN PECAN SAUCE
Ternera en Nogada

VEAL IN PRUNE SAUCE
Ternera en Salsa de Ciruelas

VEAL ST. PATRICK
Ternear San Patricio

"If Paradise isn't there, it must be close by."

Amerigo Vespucci

BEEFSTEAK FOR DESMOND GUINNESS

Biftec con Cerveza

This must be started 3 hours before you plan to eat. However, it is simple to make.

Slice the meat into strips. Sauté in butter until brown. Let stand.

Mix the beer, onion slices, tomato paste, and flour and let this stand for 2 hours. Lay the beef strips in a buttered casserole which has a lid. Pour the beer mixture and onions over all. Cover and bake in a moderate oven for ½ hour. Uncover and bake a further 20 minutes. For company: Potatoes with spinach.

Serves 4.

1½ pounds sirloin steak, sliced ½ inch thick
1 tablespoon butter
1 cup light beer
1 medium onion, sliced
1 tablespoon tomato paste
½ tablespoon all-purpose flour

BEEF MAZATLÁN

Carne de Res de Mazatlán

Cut steak into 6 equal portions, sprinkle with salt and pepper, and fry in oil and butter until well browned on both sides and cooked to your preference. Serve covered with the following sauce:

Heat 2 tablespoons of the butter and the olive oil in a skillet. Sauté carrot, onion, garlic, oregano, and bay leaf until the onion is brown—about 5 minutes. Sprinkle in the flour and cook until the flour is golden brown—about another 5 minutes. Add tomato puree, chile powder, green pepper, and salt and cook slowly, stirring occasionally, for half an hour. Just before pouring over the meat, stir in remaining tablespoon of butter. For company: *Rajas con Queso* and Mexican rice.

Serves 6.

3 pounds sirloin steak
Salt and pepper to taste
2 tablespoons butter
2 tablespoons olive oil
3 tablespoons butter
1 tablespoon olive oil
1 carrot, scraped and sliced
1 onion, chopped
2 cloves garlic, finely chopped
½ teaspoon oregano
1 bay leaf, crumbled
2 tablespoons flour
3 cups tomato puree
1½ teaspoons chile powder
1 small green pepper, chopped
½ teaspoon salt

RUM HASH

Picadillo con Ron

Use a pot large enough for all the ingredients. Dissolve the tomato paste in water. Add the peppers, onions, and oil. Cook over medium heat for 15 minutes. Add the rum and the ground meat, which *must* be very lean. Stir well while cooking (to prevent sticking) until most of the liquid has evaporated—about 1 hour. Add salt and pepper, then the chile powder. Cook a few minutes longer until the meat is almost dry. Transfer the meat into a baking dish and bake in a low oven until a tender crust has been formed—about 20 minutes. For company: *Frijoles* and Green Beans with Green Peppers. Serves 8.

2 cans tomato paste
1 cup water
3 bell peppers, seeded and chopped
2 large onions, chopped
½ cup corn oil
½ cup light rum
4 pounds lean ground beef
Salt and pepper to taste
1 teaspoon chile powder

TAMPICO STEAKS

Carne Asada a la Tampiqueña

Rub the steaks with olive oil; sprinkle with salt and pepper. Broil to your degree of preference. Serve with *Rajas con Queso, Frijoles Refritos*, Guacamole, and 1 beef or cheese enchilada per person. Serves 6.

6 shell steaks, ½ inch thick
2 tablespoons olive oil
½ lemon
Salt and pepper to taste

RED-HOT BEEFSTEAK AND MUSHROOMS

Biftec con Chipotles y Hongos

Cut the onion in half and slice it. Sauté the onion slices in lard until soft. Remove and set aside. Turn up the heat and, in the same pan, sear the steak on both sides to seal in the juices. Seed the chiles and put in a blender with the tomatoes to puree. Combine this puree with the onions and salt and pour over the steaks in a baking dish. Bake in low oven, covered, for 1 hour and 20 minutes. Add the mushrooms and continue to bake for 10 minutes. Serves 4.

1 onion
3 tablespoons lard
2 pounds round steak
3 *chipotles* or yellow chiles in vinegar
1 cup peeled, seeded, and chopped tomatoes
1 teaspoon salt
½ pound mushrooms, sliced

MEAT LOAF IN HAZELNUT SAUCE

Lomo en Salsa de Avellanas

Grind the dry hazelnuts in the blender. Grind the two kinds of meat together or ask your butcher to do it. Combine the ground meat with the olives, onion, chiles, eggs, salt, and pepper. Shape this into a loaf and wrap a thin cloth around it, tying it securely. Place in a pot with 2 cups of water and the bay leaf, thyme, marjoram, and oregano. Cover and cook, simmering, for 2 hours. Remove to a platter and unwrap; keep warm in a low oven. Reserve the broth. In 2 tablespoons melted butter brown the cornstarch, then add the hazelnuts, the stock, and salt and pepper to taste. Cook over medium heat, stirring occasionally. When the sauce begins to thicken, add the sherry. Over a low heat bring the sauce to a boil then pour over the meat loaf and serve.

Serves 6.

1⅓ cups blanched hazelnuts
½ pound pork loin, ground
1 pound veal, ground
12 pimiento-stuffed olives, sliced
1 medium onion, chopped
2 *jalapeño* chiles, seeded and chopped
2 raw eggs
1 teaspoon salt
¼ teaspoon pepper
1 bay leaf
½ teaspoon each thyme, marjoram, and oregano
2 tablespoons butter
1 tablespoon cornstarch
1 cup stock
Salt and pepper to taste
¼ cup dry sherry

MEATBALLS ABOUNDING

Albóndigas

Ask your butcher to grind the meats together, blending them well. Remove the casings from the *chorizos* and chop. Combine the ground meat, sausage, chicken, onions, eggs, olives, salt, pepper, chiles, and chile powder very thoroughly. Wrap this in a thin cloth and tied securely. Place the bundle in a pot of boiling water just to cover; add the vinegar, bay leaves, thyme, marjoram, and oregano, and cook at a low boil for 2 hours. Remove the loaf from the liquid, unwrap carefully, and serve sliced. For company: *Ensalada de Aguacate* and *Frijoles Refritos*. Serves 8.

1 pound lean ground beef
1 pound lean ground pork
3 *chorizos* (sausages)
1 chicken breast, cooked and chopped
2 onions, finely chopped
4 eggs
1 cup chopped pitted green olives
Salt and pepper to taste
3 *jalapeño* chiles, seeded and chopped
2 teaspoons chile powder
2 cups vinegar
2 bay leaves
1 teaspoon thyme
½ teaspoon each marjoram and oregano

BEEF STEW

Estofado de Res

Brown the meat in hot lard with the garlic clove. Remove the garlic, add the onion, and sauté until soft. Add the broth and seasonings, cover, and cook slowly until the meat is tender—1¼ to 1½ hours. Add the green peppers and tomatoes and cook another 30 minutes. Add the potatoes and cook ½ hour longer. Add zucchini in half slices and cook until tender—about 10 minutes. In all, about 2½ hours' cooking time. Serves 6.

1½ pounds lean beef, cubed
2 tablespoons lard
1 clove garlic
1 large onion, chopped
2 cups beef broth
1 bay leaf
½ teaspoon each thyme and oregano
Salt and pepper to taste
2 green peppers, seeded and chopped
3 large tomatoes, peeled, seeded, and chopped
3 medium potatoes, peeled, cut into sixths
2 large zucchini

UPHOLSTERED LEG OF LAMB

Pierna de Carnero Estofado

Prepare the chiles as in Part II, Stage One. Make 6 incisions in the leg of lamb and insert the garlic slivers. Sprinkle all over with salt and pepper. Put the lamb in a heavy casserole with a lid.

Put the quartered tomatoes, onion, chiles with water and sugar in a blender and blend to a *coarse* puree. Sauté the puree in lard over moderate heat for 5 minutes, stirring constantly. Add the chicken stock and stir. Pour this sauce over the leg of lamb, seal the casserole with aluminum foil, and cover with the lid. Cook in a moderate oven for 3½ hours. Serve with rice which has been cooked in equal parts of water and sauce from the lamb casserole. Serves 8.

6 *ancho* chiles
1 4-pound leg of lamb
2 cloves garlic, slivered
Salt and pepper to taste
2 medium tomatoes, peeled, seeded, and quartered
1 large onion, roughly chopped
1 teaspoon sugar
2 tablespoons lard or corn oil
2 cups chicken stock

TWELVE-FLAVORED LAMB

Adobo de Carnero

Prepare the chiles as in Part II, Stage One. If *mulato* chiles are not available, use all *ancho* chiles. Place the lamb in a heavy lidded casserole. Add half the onions, 1 clove garlic, 1 teaspoon salt, and the pepper, thyme, marjoram, bay leaves, and parsley. Add enough water to barely cover the lamb, cover, and bring to a boil. Reduce heat and cook slowly for 1½ hours. Remove the lamb with a slotted spoon; strain the stock, reserving the liquid. Put the chiles, the remaining onion, garlic clove, the tomatoes, and 1 teaspoon of salt in the blender with ½ cup of stock, and puree. Heat the lard and sauté the puree for 5 minutes, stirring. Wash out the casserole, put the lamb in it, and pour the puree over it. Add 1 cup of the lamb stock, the raisins, and the peaches and cook, uncovered, over low heat for 40 minutes. For company: Sesame Rice.
Serves 6.

3 *ancho* chiles
3 *mulato* chiles
3 pounds boneless lamb in 2-inch pieces
2 onions, roughly chopped
2 cloves garlic, sliced
2 teaspoons salt
½ teaspoon pepper
1 teaspoon thyme
½ teaspoon marjoram
2 bay leaves
2 sprigs parsley
2 tomatoes, peeled, seeded, and chopped
2 tablespoons lard
2 tablespoons raisins
½ cup diced preserved peaches

PORK MOLE

Mole de Chile Serrano

Cook the pork slowly in salted water to cover for 1 hour. Drain the pork, reserving the stock, and set aside. Put tomatoes, chiles, oregano, thyme, and *epazote* into blender. Blend to a smooth puree. Heat lard in a skillet and sauté the puree for 5 minutes, stirring constantly. Add the reserved stock, bay leaves, salt and pepper to taste, and stir. Put the chicken pieces into a heavy flameproof casserole with the pork cubes. Pour the sauce over all. Cook, covered, over low heat, until the chicken is well cooked—about 1½ hours. For company: Sesame Rice and Refried Beans.
Serves 6.

1 pound boneless pork, cubed
1 pound tomatoes, peeled, seeded, and
    chopped
12 *serrano* chiles, sliced
½ teaspoon oregano
½ teaspoon thyme
1 sprig *epazote,* if available
1 tablespoon lard
2 bay leaves
Salt and pepper to taste
1 4-pound chicken, cut into serving pieces

AZTEC PORK PIE TO THE TASTE OF BIANCA JAGGER

Torta Azteca al Gusto de Bianca Jagger

Fry the pork thoroughly in 3 tablespoons of the lard. Cool slightly and grind in meat grinder. In the same skillet, using remaining lard, sauté tomatoes, onion, and garlic for 5 minutes. Add ½ cup water, ground pork, and bell peppers. Cook for 15 minutes. Meanwhile, whisk the egg whites and yolks separately and fold together. Fry the tortillas in butter until brown and dip them in the eggs. In a buttered casserole place 2 tortillas, then a layer of pork mixture, then a layer of grated cheese. Repeat. Bake for 20 minutes in a moderate oven. Serve with your favorite hot sauce.
Serves 8.

2 pounds lean pork, cubed
½ cup lard or corn oil
5 tomatoes, peeled and chopped
1 large onion, chopped
1 clove garlic, finely chopped
½ cup water
4 small bell peppers, very thinly sliced
3 eggs, separated
10 tortillas
⅓ cup butter
1 cup grated cheese

EIGHT-FLAVORED PORK

Lomo de Puerco Adobo

Slice the bacon, ham, and *jalapeños* into narrow strips. Lay the strips alternately on the pork loin in a heavy casserole with a lid. Sprinkle with salt and pepper. Put onion and garlic in a blender with orange juice and blend to a smooth puree. Add the chile powder and mix it in with the sauce. Pour this sauce over the meat, add the mashed bananas, and cook, tightly covered, in a moderate oven for 1½ hours. For company: Torta de Papas.
Serves 6.

4 slices lean bacon
3 slices boiled ham
3 *jalapeño* chiles
3 pounds pork loin
Salt and pepper
1 medium onion, roughly chopped
1 large clove garlic, crushed
1½ cups orange juice
1½ tablespoons chile powder
2 bananas, mashed

YSABEL DEIGHTON'S PIGLET

Carnitas de Puerco de Ysabel Deighton

Boil the pork slowly slowly in enough salted water to cover, for 40 minutes. Drain, then cut the meat into cubes. Heat the oil and lard in a skillet and fry the pork cubes until crisp and brown on all sides.

Carnitas may be used as a filling for tacos with guacamole or served in a *mole* sauce such as *Mole Oaxaqueño* or *Mole Poblano*, with rice and beans.
Serves 6–8.

3 pounds pork loin
1 teaspoon salt
¼ cup corn oil
4 tablespoons pork lard

VEAL IN PECAN SAUCE

Ternera en Nogada

Cook the veal with the stock, half the onions, the garlic, and the thyme in a heavy pot over low heat for 1½ hours, covered. Lift out the veal and set aside. Strain the stock and reserve it. Sauté the remaining onions in butter until soft. Add the pecans and sauté for 2 minutes. Put the onions and pecans in a blender with ½ cup veal stock and blend it until smooth. Put the remainder of the stock in a pot, add the pecan puree, salt and pepper to taste, and cook for 5 minutes. Stir in the cream, add the veal and heat through. For company: White rice and *Chícharos Chihuahua*. Serves 6.

3 pounds veal for stew, in 1-inch cubes
2 cups chicken stock
2 onions, chopped
1 large clove garlic, finely chopped
½ teaspoon thyme
2 tablespoons butter
½ cup shelled pecans
Salt and pepper to taste
1 cup heavy cream

VEAL IN PRUNE SAUCE

Ternera en Salsa de Ciruelas

Soak prunes in wine for 4 hours. If they are not pitted, cut the meat off the pit after 2 hours of soaking and chop it. Melt the butter and sauté the chops until brown on both sides over moderate heat. Place in a fireproof dish or casserole with a lid. Sauté the onions in the same skillet with remaining butter until soft. Mix in garlic, tomatoes, nutmeg, and salt and pepper. Smother the chops with this mixture, cover, and cook over low heat for 1¼ to 1½ hours. Combine prunes and wine with the chops and cook another 15 minutes, uncovered. Serve with rice and *Ensalada Noche Buena*.
Serves 6.

At Rossenarra, on the *altiplano* of County Kilkenny, we discovered that the Irish didn't sell pitted prunes. When I started to try to remove the prune pits I found the prunes most reluctant to give them up. As there were a lot of other things to do, I decided to leave the job until later. After two hours of soaking in wine, it was much easier to get them out though it still called for a sharp knife to cut the prune away from the pit. Still, by that time, with all that hacking, the prunes were nearly chopped.

1 cup large pitted prunes, chopped
1 cup red wine
4 tablespoons butter
6 large veal chops
2 onions, finely chopped
1 clove garlic, finely chopped
1 pound tomatoes, peeled, seeded, and chopped
½ teaspoon ground nutmeg
Salt and pepper to taste

VEAL ST. PATRICK

Ternera San Patricio

Cook veal in enough water to cover in a heavy pot with 1 teaspoon salt. Bring to a boil, then reduce heat and simmer until tender when tested with a fork—about 1½ hours. Drain and reserve stock. Place onion, garlic, chiles, coriander, lettuce, and almonds in a blender with water and puree. To achieve a smooth puree will take 2 to 3 minutes. Melt the butter in a skillet and cook the puree, stirring constantly, for 5 minutes. Add enough veal stock to get a sauce with the consistency of thick cream. Pour the sauce over the veal, or if there is room add the veal to the sauce, with salt and pepper to taste, and heat through, but do not boil. Serve with rice. For company: *Chícharos Norteños.*
Serves 4.

This dish originally called for green tomatoes, but we had to import them to Rossenarra and I had run out. However, the improvisation is so delicious that I can only recommend it as above.

3 pounds boneless veal cut in cubes
1 teaspoon salt
1 large onion, chopped
1 large or 2 small cloves garlic, chopped
2 *jalapeño* chiles, sliced
½ teaspoon ground coriander, or 5 sprigs fresh
1½ cups chopped green lettuce
¼ cup blanched almonds
¼ cup water
4 tablespoons butter
Salt and pepper to taste

"It has always pleased me to exalt plants on the scale of organized beings."

Charles Darwin, *Autobiography*

VEGETABLES AND SALAD
LEGUMBRES Y ENSALADAS

AVOCADO SALAD
Ensalada de Aguacate

BELL PEPPERS STUFFED WITH NUT SAUCE
Chiles en Nogada Estilo Puebla

CAULIFLOWER PUEBLA STYLE
Coliflor Estilo Puebla

CHIAPAS SALAD
Ensalada de Chiapas

HARLEQUIN POTATOES
Papas Arlequinescas

JUÁREZ SALAD
Ensalada Juárez

LIMA BEANS WITH CREAM CHEESE
Habas con Queso

LEMON-POTATO CAKE
Torta de Papas con Limón

LENTILS WITH PORK
Lentejas con Puerco

PEPPER STRIPS WITH CREAM CHEESE
Rajas con Queso

PEAS OF THE NORTH
Chícharos Norteños

PESADUMBRE

CHRISTMAS EVE SALAD
Ensalada de Nochebuena

SWEET POTATOES AND FRUIT
Camote con Fruta

STRING BEANS WITH GREEN PEPPERS
Ejotes con Rajas

STUFFED BELL PEPPERS
Chiles Rellenos

ZUCCHINI SOUTHERN STYLE
Calabacitas Tehuantepec

ZUCCHINI AND AVOCADO SALAD
Ensalada de Calabacitas y Aguacate

AVOCADO SALAD

Ensalada de Aguacate

Arrange the avocados, tomatoes, and onions in a dish. Make a dressing of lemon juice and olive oil with mustard, garlic, salt, and pepper.

3 avocados, sliced
2 large tomatoes, peeled and sliced
1 large onion, sliced
¼ cup lemon juice
½ cup olive oil
½ teaspoon dry mustard
1 clove garlic, pressed
Salt and pepper to taste

BELL PEPPERS STUFFED WITH NUT SAUCE

Chiles en Nogada Estilo Puebla

Singe the peppers under the broiler, wrap them in a damp cloth for ½ hour, then remove the skins. Slit the peppers lengthwise and remove the seeds, then soak them in a quart of water with 1 tablespoon salt for 20 minutes. Drain well and stuff with the following mixture.

Fry the onion and garlic in lard until the onion is soft. Add the ground pork and cook until done. Add ½ cup of the ground walnuts, 1 cup hot water, parsley, apples, peaches, raisins, cinnamon, half the cloves, pepper, sugar, and the sherry. Simmer until the liquid has evaporated—about 10 minutes.

Pour the sauce made from the following over the hot stuffed peppers: blend thoroughly the remaining ½ cup of ground walnuts, cream cheese, broiled chopped garlic, remaining cloves, cumin, salt to taste, and the milk (use additional milk if the sauce is too thick). The sauce should have the consistency of heavy cream. Sprinkle the pomegranate seeds over all. Serves 6.

6 large bell peppers
1 medium onion, finely chopped
2 cloves garlic, finely chopped
2 tablespoons lard
1 pound ground pork
1 cup ground walnuts
1 cup hot water
1 tablespoon finely chopped parsley
1 apple, peeled, cored, and chopped
2 peaches, peeled and chopped
⅓ cup seedless raisins
1 teaspoon ground cinnamon
½ teaspoon ground cloves
Pepper to taste
1 tablespoon sugar
¼ cup sherry
½ cup cream cheese
1 garlic clove, broiled and finely chopped
¼ teaspoon ground cumin
Salt to taste
½ cup milk
Seeds from 1 pomegranate

CAULIFLOWER PUEBLA STYLE

Coliflor Estilo Puebla

Break the cauliflower into flowerets and cook in boiling salted water for 15 minutes. Drain. Gently sauté the tomatoes, pimiento, onion, chile, and parsley in lard for 15 minutes. Add cloves, cinnamon, bay leaves, salt, and pepper and cook for 5 more minutes. Add the chopped olives and capers and allow the sauce to cool. Remove cloves, cinnamon, and bay leaves. Pour two thirds of the sauce in a baking dish, lay cauliflower over this, and cover the flowerets with the remaining sauce. Sprinkle the bread crumbs over the top, then the grated cheese, and dot with butter. Bake in a moderate oven for 10 minutes.

Serves 6.

1 medium head cauliflower
3 tomatoes, chopped
½ pimiento, chopped
1 medium onion, chopped
1 *jalapeño* chile, seeded and chopped
3 teaspoons chopped parsley
4 tablespoons lard
2 cloves
1 stick cinnamon
2 bay leaves
Salt and pepper to taste
2 stuffed olives, chopped
1 tablespoon capers
3 tablespoons bread crumbs
4 tablespoons grated cheese
A little butter

CHIAPAS SALAD

Ensalada de Chiapas

Scrape the celery thoroughly. Mash the avocado, cream cheese, and banana. Thinly slice the celery and mix with the sugar, lemon juice, and salt; add to the mashed ingredients. Chill and serve on lettuce sprinkled with walnuts.
Serves 6.

6 stalks celery
1 large avocado
1 ounce cream cheese
1 banana
1 teaspoon sugar
2 tablespoons lemon juice
Salt to taste
Lettuce
5 tablespoons chopped walnuts

HARLEQUIN POTATOES

Papas Arlequinescas

Brown the raw potatoes in lard. Add garlic, cayenne pepper, ginger, and salt. Sauté, stirring for 2 minutes, then add the chopped spinach. Mix these together thoroughly. If the spinach does not provide enough moisture, add ¼ cup hot water. Cover and cook slowly until the potatoes are done—about 20 minutes.
Serves 4.

3 medium potatoes, peeled and quartered
8 tablespoons lard
2 cloves garlic, finely chopped
¼ teaspoon cayenne pepper
1 teaspoon ground ginger
1 teaspoon salt
1 pound spinach, chopped

JUÁREZ SALAD

Ensalada de Juárez

Blend all ingredients except the lettuce. Chill and serve on the lettuce.
Serves 4.

1 cup canned white kernel corn
1 cup chopped walnuts
2 green peppers, chopped
¾ cup sour cream
3 tablespoons lemon juice
1 teaspoon sugar
⅓ cup olive oil
1 teaspoon salt
Lettuce

LIMA BEANS WITH CREAM CHEESE

Habas con Queso

Cook the lima beans in boiling salted water for 25 to 30 minutes. Drain them well and keep them warm. Sauté the onion and the garlic in butter until the onion is soft. Add the tomatoes and the chile and salt and pepper to taste. Simmer the mixture for 10 minutes, stirring occasionally. Add the sliced cream cheese and cook for 5 more minutes, stirring. Pour this over the lima beans and mix together.
Serves 6.

1½ pounds green lima beans, shelled
Salt
1 medium onion, finely chopped
2 cloves garlic, chopped
2 tablespoons butter
2 medium tomatoes, peeled, seeded, and chopped
1 *jalapeño* chile, chopped
Pepper to taste
8 ounces cream cheese, sliced

LEMON-POTATO CAKE

Torta de Papas con Limón

Peel, boil, and mash the potatoes. Stir in other ingredients and spoon into a buttered baking dish. Bake in a moderate oven for ½ hour.
Serves 4.

1½ pounds potatoes
½ cup butter
⅓ cup sugar
3 eggs, beaten
2 teaspoons lemon rind

LENTILS WITH PORK

Lentejas con Puerco

Cook the pork cubes in enough water to barely cover, bring to a boil, cover, and simmer for 45 minutes. Drain, reserving the stock, and set aside. Drain and rinse lentils. In a clean saucepan put stock, lentils, raisins, and water to cover. Bring to a boil, cover, then simmer for 40 minutes. Drain and set aside. Twenty minutes before lentils are done, fry pork, onion, and garlic in oil until pork is lightly browned. Add to the lentils. In the same oil, with butter added, sauté apple, banana, and pineapple for a few minutes; then add tomatoes and salt and pepper to taste, and cook until most of the liquid has evaporated. Combine all ingredients and simmer for 10 more minutes.
Serves 6–8.

½ pound pork, cut into small cubes
½ pound lentils, presoaked for 8 hours
¼ cup raisins
1 medium onion, finely chopped
2 cloves garlic, finely chopped
3 tablespoons olive oil
1 tablespoon butter
1 apple, peeled, cored, and chopped
1 large banana, sliced
2 cups pineapple in chunks
3 tomatoes, peeled, seeded, and chopped
Salt and pepper to taste

PEPPER STRIPS WITH CREAM CHEESE

Rajas con Queso

Slightly singe peppers under broiler. Remove stems and seeds. Cut the peppers into long, thin strips. Put tomatoes in boiling water for 2 to 3 minutes, then peel and chop. In hot fat, fry onions until golden brown. Add the peppers, tomatoes, ¼ cup hot water, and salt. Simmer gently. When mixture reaches a boil, add the sliced cheese and simmer, stirring occasionally, for 10 minutes.

4 large bell peppers
4 medium tomatoes
3 tablespoons lard or corn oil
2 onions, sliced
¼ cup hot water
1 teaspoon salt
8 ounces cream cheese, sliced

PEAS OF THE NORTH

Chícharos Norteños

Cook the peas in 1 cup salted water. Drain and set aside. Melt 4 tablespoons of the butter in a heavy enameled casserole with a lid. Put the carrots, potato, onions, lettuce hearts, herbs, with salt and pepper to taste in casserole. Stir and cover. Cook without water over low heat for 25 minutes. Mix flour with cream. Add the cooked peas, remaining 3 tablespoons butter, and flour-cream mixture. Stir to blend thoroughly, cover, and cook slowly for 10 minutes more.
Serves 6.

2 pounds fresh or frozen peas
7 tablespoons butter
2 medium carrots, scraped and diced
1 medium potato, scraped and diced
2 medium onions, finely chopped
2 lettuce hearts, sliced
1 bay leaf
⅛ teaspoon thyme
⅛ teaspoon marjoram
⅛ teaspoon oregano
Salt and pepper to taste
1 tablespoon flour
½ pint light cream

PESADUMBRE

Cook vegetables separately in salted water. Be sure not to overcook. Drain and put in a bowl. Mix chile powder, garlic, thyme, and cumin with vinegar. Pour over the vegetables, add salt and bay, and toss gently. Cover bowl and let mixture sit for 2 days. Chill for 3 hours before serving. Mix in the olive oil and decorate with onion rings.

2 pounds zucchini, sliced
½ pound green peas, frozen or fresh
1 pound new potatoes, peeled and halved
3 tablespoons chile powder
2 cloves garlic, pressed or finely chopped
1 teaspoon thyme
¼ teaspoon ground cumin
1 cup vinegar
½ teaspoon salt
1 bay leaf, crumbled
⅓ cup olive oil
1 onion, sliced

CHRISTMAS EVE SALAD

Ensalada de Nochebuena

Mix chilled beets, oranges, apples, bananas, and sugar cane. Mix the sugar and vinegar and blend with the fruits. Sprinkle with chopped peanuts. Serves 8.

3 medium beets, cooked and chopped
3 oranges, peeled and sectioned
3 tart apples or *jícamas,* peeled and sliced
3 bananas, peeled and sliced
1 stick sugar cane, peeled and chopped
   (optional)
½ cup sugar
3 tablespoons vinegar
½ cup chopped peanuts

SWEET POTATOES AND FRUIT

Camote con Fruta

In a shallow buttered baking dish, alternately layer sweet-potato and apple slices until both are used up. Mix the orange and lime juice with the ginger and pour over the casserole. Dot with butter and brown sugar. Sprinkle over with cinnamon. Bake in a moderate oven for ½ hour.
Serves 6.

2 medium sweet potatoes, cooked, peeled, and sliced
2 green or yellow apples, cored, peeled, and sliced
¼ cup fresh orange juice
2 tablespoons lime juice
¼ teaspoon ground ginger
3 tablespoons butter
3 tablespoons brown sugar
½ teaspoon ground cinnamon

STRING BEANS WITH GREEN PEPPERS

Ejotes con Rajas

Cut the beans in long strips or use French-cut frozen string beans. Cook until not quite tender and drain. Cut the onion in half lengthwise and slice it. Sauté the onion slices in butter in a large skillet until soft but not brown. Add green peppers. Add the drained string beans. Cover and simmer until pepper strips are tender—about 5 minutes. Salt and pepper to taste.
Serves 6.

1½ pounds green beans
1 small onion
3 tablespoons butter
3 green peppers, sliced into thin strips
Salt and pepper to taste

STUFFED BELL PEPPERS

Chiles Rellenos

Singe the peppers under a broiler. Wrap them in a damp cloth for ½ hour. Peel the skin off and cut lengthwise, carefully removing all the seeds. Put the tomatoes in the blender and puree. Brown onion and ground meat in lard. Add the pureed tomatoes, almonds, raisins, parsley, cinnamon, salt, and pepper. Add the hot water and simmer, stirring occasionally, for 25 minutes. Stuff the peppers with this filling. Beat the egg whites and yolks separately and fold them together. Coat the stuffed peppers in flour, then dip each one into the eggs. Fry in deep fat until golden. Drain and serve.
Serves 6.

6 bell peppers
½ pound tomatoes, peeled and quartered
1 onion, chopped
½ pound ground pork
½ pound ground veal
2 tablespoons lard
⅓ cup blanched, slivered almonds
2 tablespoons seedless raisins
1 teaspoon chopped parsley
½ teaspoon ground cinnamon
Salt and pepper to taste
⅓ cup hot water
3 eggs, separated
All-purpose flour
1 cup corn oil

ZUCCHINI SOUTHERN STYLE

Calabacitas Tehuantepec

Fry the pork bits until browned in 1 tablespoon of the lard. Set aside. Fry zucchini, onions, tomatoes, chile, and peppers together gently in the remaining 3 tablespoons lard until the zucchini is tender—about 15 minutes. Stir in the pork bits and add salt and pepper to taste. Top with grated cheese before serving.

⅓ pound pork, chopped
4 tablespoons lard
6 medium zucchini, chopped
2 medium onions, chopped
3 medium tomatoes, peeled and chopped
1 *serrano* chile, finely chopped
2 bell peppers, seeded and chopped
1 cup grated cheese

ZUCCHINI AND AVOCADO SALAD

Ensalada de Calabacitas y Aguacate

Cut the tops off the zucchini and slice in half lengthwise. Scoop out the insides; reserve shells. In a bowl, stir together the zucchini cores, avocados, onion, mint, and celery. Make a dressing of oil, vinegar, and garlic with salt and pepper. Pour over the vegetables and mix well. Spoon this into the zucchini shells and chill. Garnish with lettuce and quartered hard-boiled eggs.
Serves 6.

6 medium zucchini, parboiled
2 avocados, peeled and diced
1 small onion, chopped
6 mint leaves, chopped
1 stalk celery, finely chopped
4 tablespoons olive oil
1 tablespoon vinegar
1 clove garlic, finely chopped
Salt and pepper to taste
Lettuce
Hard-boiled eggs

RICE AND BEANS
ARROZ Y FRIJOLES

"If you're always ready, you're always glad."

Franklin M. Heller, Municipal Fromagist,
Pickering City, Texas (1814–71)

CROWN OF RICE
Corona de Arroz

GREEN RICE
Arroz Verde

MEXICAN RICE
Arroz Mexicano

NICE SPICY RICE CORNELIA
Arroz Adobo

SESAME RICE MIRZA
Arroz Ajonjolí Mirza

STRAIGHT-DOWN RICE
Arroz del Sur

TABASCO RICE
Arroz Tabasqueño

MEXICAN BEANS
Frijoles Mexicanos

RANCHERS' BEANS
Frijoles Rancheros

REFRIED BEANS
Frijoles Refritos

Before proceeding, be certain to consult how to make Mexican Beans in Part II, Stage One.

CROWN OF RICE

Corona de Arroz

Soak the rice in hot water for 15 minutes, rinse until the water runs clear, then drain well. Fry the rice in hot oil with the onion until both are golden. Pour off excess oil and add the hot water. Simmer a few minutes until the liquid is absorbed. Add the milk and salt. Cover and simmer over low heat until almost dry—about 15 minutes. Take off heat and add 4 tablespoons of the butter in small chunks. Sprinkle a buttered ring mold with bread crumbs. Pack in a layer of rice, lay on the cheese slices and little chunks of butter, followed by a final layer of rice, and pack this down. Bake the mold in a moderate oven for 10 minutes. Turn out onto a serving plate and garnish with carrots, peas, and hard-boiled egg slices. Fill the center with Guacamole. Serves 6.

1 cup short-grain rice
½ cup corn oil
1 medium onion, chopped
½ cup hot water
2 cups milk
1 tablespoon salt
8 tablespoons butter
¼ cup bread crumbs
3 ounces Swiss cheese, sliced
2 ounces American cheese, sliced
1 medium carrot, cooked and sliced
1 small can baby peas, heated and drained
1 hard-boiled egg, sliced
2 cups Guacamole

GREEN RICE

Arroz Verde

Puree the bell peppers, onion, parsley, garlic, and chiles with ½ cup of the stock. Soak the rice for 15 minutes in hot water to cover. Rinse well in cold water and drain thoroughly. Fry the rice in hot oil until golden. Add the puree and sauté, stirring, for 5 minutes. Pour the rice mixture into a pot with the stock and salt and pepper. Bring to a boil, then cook, covered, over a low heat until all the liquid has been absorbed.
Serves 8.

4 bell peppers, seeded and chopped
1 medium onion, chopped
¼ cup parsley sprigs
2 cloves garlic, sliced
2 fresh green chiles or canned *serrano* chiles
4 cups chicken stock
2 cups short-grain rice
¼ cup corn oil
Salt and pepper to taste

MEXICAN RICE

Arroz Mexicano

Soak the rice in enough hot water to cover for 15 minutes, then rinse thoroughly in cold water until the water runs clear. Drain well. Puree tomatoes, onion, and garlic in a blender. Fry *chorizo* slices in lard for 5 minutes. Lift out and set aside. In the same fat, fry the rice until golden. Pour off excess fat and add the tomato-onion-garlic puree. Sauté this with the rice for 5 minutes. Transfer this mixture to a saucepan and add 1 cup of the stock. Bring to a boil, then lower heat and simmer, covered, until almost dry. Add the remaining stock and the salt and continue cooking until the liquid has been absorbed. Just before it is done, stir in the peas. Turn into a warm serving dish and top with avocado slices and sausage.
Serves 8.

2 cups short-grain rice
1½ cups tomatoes, peeled, seeded, and chopped
1 large onion
2 cloves garlic
2 *chorizo* sausages, sliced (optional)
½ cup lard or corn oil
4 cups chicken stock
¾ teaspoon salt
½ cup cooked peas
1 avocado, peeled and sliced

NICE SPICY RICE CORNELIA

Arroz Adobo

Puree the tomatoes in a blender with salt. Fry the onions in oil until soft. Add the garlic, ginger, cloves, coriander, and pepper. Sauté, stirring, for 2 minutes. Add the rice and fry all together until rice is golden. Put all this in a pot with the boiling water; stir in tomatoes. Cover and cook over a low heat for about 20 minutes—until almost all the liquid has been absorbed.
Serves 8.

1½ cups peeled, seeded, and quartered tomatoes
1½ teaspoons salt
2 medium onions, chopped
¼ cup oil or lard
3 cloves garlic, finely chopped
½ teaspoon ground ginger
¼ teaspoon ground cloves
¼ teaspoon ground coriander
¼ teaspoon pepper
2 cups rice
3½ cups boiling water

SESAME RICE MIRZA

Arroz Ajonjolí Mirza

Cook rice in boiling salted water for 20 minutes. Sauté the pecans for 5 minutes in 1 tablespoon of the butter. Remove pecans and set aside. Add the remaining butter and fry the sesame seeds, cayenne, and bay until the sesame seeds are golden brown. Combine pecans and sesame mixture. Stir into hot, cooked rice. Sprinkle with lime juice.

1 cup long-grain rice
2½ cups boiling water
1 teaspoon salt
3 tablespoons pecan halves
2 tablespoons butter
1 cup sesame seeds
½ teaspoon cayenne pepper
1 bay leaf, crumbled
1 tablespoon lime juice (optional) (Rose's unsweetened lime juice may be used)

STRAIGHT-DOWN RICE

Arroz del Sur

Soak the rice in hot water for 15 minutes. Rinse thoroughly in cold water and drain well. Fry the rice in 2 tablespoons of the butter and the olive oil until golden. Add garlic, onion, peas, and 1 teaspoon salt. Mix this well, sauté a few minutes longer, then drain off any excess fat. Add half of the water and simmer over low heat. When all the water has been absorbed, add remaining water and ¼ cup of the cream. Cover and cook slowly until rice is nearly dry. Add shrimp and tunafish and stir together. Transfer the rice to a buttered casserole and stand the casserole in a pan of hot water. Bake in a very low oven while making the sauce: Melt remaining 3 tablespoons butter in a saucepan. Add remaining ¼ cup cream, catsup, and salt and pepper to taste. Simmer, stirring, for 3 minutes. Pour over rice and cover with pimiento strips.

1 cup short-grain rice
5 tablespoons butter
2 tablespoons olive oil
2 large cloves garlic, finely chopped
1 medium onion, finely chopped
1 cup cooked baby peas
1 teaspoon salt
1¼ cups hot water
½ cup light cream
½ cup shrimp
½ cup tunafish
1 cup catsup
Salt and pepper to taste
2 pimientos, cut into strips

TABASCO RICE

Arroz Tabasqueño

Cook rice according to instructions on package. Dissolve the saffron in 2 tablespoons hot water. Add the egg and mix well. In the oil fry onion, garlic, tomato, bell pepper, capers, bananas, apples, salt, and hard-boiled eggs for 5 minutes. Add the saffron-egg mixture to rice and blend well. In a casserole put half the rice, then the sautéed fruit and vegetables, then cover with the remaining rice. Dot the top with lumps of butter and bake for 15 minutes in a moderate oven.
Serves 6.

1 cup long-grain rice, cooked
¼ teaspoon saffron
2 tablespoons hot water
1 egg
4 tablespoons corn oil
1 small onion, chopped
2 cloves garlic, chopped
1 medium tomato, peeled and chopped
1 bell pepper, chopped
1 tablespoon capers
2 firm bananas, sliced
2 apples, peeled, cored, and chopped
½ teaspoon salt
2 hard-boiled eggs, chopped
3 tablespoons butter

MEXICAN BEANS

Frijoles Mexicanos

Clean the beans with plenty of running water, removing all foreign matter. Soak them for 8 hours before cooking. Put the beans to boil with water to cover, adding the onion. An earthenware flameproof pot is best to use. When the skins begin to wrinkle add 1 tablespoon of the lard and the *epazote* and cover the pot. The beans should simmer slowly. As the liquid is absorbed, add more hot water. After 3½ hours of cooking, add 1½ teaspoons salt and cook until the beans are very soft—about 45 minutes. Strain the broth into a large bowl, mash 3 tablespoons of the beans, and stir these into the broth. Cook the remainder of the beans in remaining tablespoon of lard, strain the bean stock again, and pour it over the beans. Season with salt and pepper and simmer until very thick—about 20 minutes.

1 cup pink, red, or black kidney beans
4 quarts water
1 onion
2 tablespoons lard
1 sprig *epazote*, if available
1½ teaspoons salt
Pepper to taste

RANCHERS' BEANS

Frijoles Rancheros

Combine all ingredients and cook for 20 minutes.

1 cup cooked *frijoles*
2 *jalapeño* chiles, seeded and chopped
2 tomatoes, peeled, seeded, and chopped
2 cloves garlic, finely chopped
½ teaspoon ground cinnamon
⅛ teaspoon ground cloves
1 onion, chopped
2 tablespoons olive oil
Juice of 1 lemon
1 teaspoon salt

REFRIED BEANS

Frijoles Refritos

Cook the beans as directed in recipe for Mexican Beans, taking care to remove the *epazote* when beans are fully cooked. Mash the beans or put half the beans in a blender and mash only half of them, combining the mash with the blended beans. Heat lard in a skillet and add the mashed beans. Stir occasionally, turning the beans well until they reach a heavy, thick constituency and are quite dry. Roll the beans up like an omelet and sprinkle with grated cheese.

Refried beans go with everything but the dessert. Next to the tortilla, which often shows up in desserts, this is the greatest Mexican staple.

EGGS *HUEVOS*

EGGS ELENORA MÍA
Huevos Exquisitos

EGGS HA MAT SUN*
Jinetes a Caballo con Chaparreras

RANCHERS' EGGS
Huevos Rancheros

MEXICAN SCRAMBLED EGGS
Huevos Revueltos a la Mexicana

---

* Ha Mat Sun, who was most probably the inventor of *chile con carne,* was head chuckwagon cook for the Gus Peters Adelphi ranch at Buckingham, Texas, between 1844 and 1871.

EGGS ELENORA MÍA

Huevos Exquisitos

Cook the beans as in *Frijoles Mexicanos*, then mash and fry them in 1 tablespoon of the lard. Fry the tortillas in lard and drain. Fry the eggs one by one. Sauté onion and peppers in 1 tablespoon of the lard. Add the tomato puree and let simmer until thickened. Put a layer of beans and 1 egg on each tortilla, cover with sauce, sprinkle with cheese, and serve hot.

¾ cup boiled beans
6 tablespoons lard
6 tortillas
6 eggs
1 cup tomato puree
1 onion, chopped
2 bell peppers, toasted, cleaned, sliced
2 tablespoons grated cheese

EGGS HA MAT SUN

Jinetes a Caballo con Chaparreras

Boil the pork with 1 of the onions, the bay, and the thyme. When it has cooked about 1 hour, put it into a blender and grind it with the *chipotle* chiles and the cream. Season with salt and pepper. Roast the tomatoes and grind together with the other onion, *serrano* chiles, and coriander; with a wooden spoon, mix these with mashed avocados and tomato mixture. Season with salt and pepper. Brown the toasted tortillas in lard. Fry the eggs. On each tortilla spread a layer of the ground-pork mixture, 2 fried eggs, one at each end, and between these a mound of the guacamole. Sprinkle with the cheese and top with a slice of radish.

1 pound pork loin
2 onions
1 bay leaf, crumbled
1 sprig thyme
2 pickled *chipotle* chiles
½ cup heavy cream
Salt and pepper to taste
2 tomatoes
2 *serrano* chiles
1 tablespoon chopped coriander
3 avocados
6 toasted tortillas with baked skins scraped off
1 cup lard
12 eggs
2 ounces fresh cheese, crumbled
1 large radish, sliced

RANCHERS' EGGS

Huevos Rancheros

Fry each tortilla in lard, just until soft, taking care not to brown them. Fry the eggs. Place each egg on a tortilla, being careful not to break the yolk. The sauce: Combine onion, garlic, chiles, and tomato puree and sauté all of it in 1 tablespoon lard. Season with salt and let simmer until slightly thickened. Pour 1 tablespoonful sauce over each egg. Garnish with slices of cheese and avocado. Serve immediately. Ranchers' Eggs may be made with scrambled eggs even more successfully because the heat of scrambled eggs may be controlled more readily.

6 tortillas
About 1½ cups lard
6 eggs
1 onion, finely chopped
1 clove garlic, finely chopped
2 small hot green *serrano* chiles to taste
1 cup tomato puree
Salt to taste
3 ounces fresh cheese
2 avocados

MEXICAN SCRAMBLED EGGS

Huevos Revueltos a la Mexicana

Sauté onion, garlic, and chiles in the lard. Add the tomato puree and season to taste. Let simmer for about 5 minutes, then add to the lightly beaten eggs. Scramble and serve immediately.

1 small onion, chopped
1 clove garlic, chopped
1½ hot *serrano* chiles, or to taste, chopped
2 tablespoons lard
½ cup tomato puree
Salt and pepper to taste
5 eggs, lightly beaten

SAUCES *SALSAS*

"O'Toole is on the sauce again!"

Tom Moore, Mayor
Kilmoganny, Co. Kilkenny, Ireland

COOKED TOMATO SAUCE
Salsa Frita

DRUNKARD'S SAUCE
Salsa Borracha

FISH SAUCE
Salsa para Pescado

GREEN SAUCE
Salsa Verde

GUACAMOLE

MEXICAN SAUCE
Salsa Mexicana

PUMPKIN-SEED SAUCE
Salsa Pipián

COOKED TOMATO SAUCE

Salsa Frita

Heat the fat in a skillet and fry the onion with the garlic until soft. Add the tomatoes and chiles and cook, stirring occasionally, for 15 minutes. Add the salt and coriander and remove from heat. This sauce may be served either hot or cold. It is especially good with eggs and goes well with hamburgers or meat loaf.

2 tablespoons lard
1 onion, cut up
1 large clove garlic
1 pound tomatoes, peeled, seeded, and chopped
2 or 3 *serrano* chiles, chopped
1 teaspoon salt
2 sprigs fresh coriander or parsley, chopped

DRUNKARD'S SAUCE

Salsa Borracha

Remove the veins and seeds from the chiles, tear them into pieces, and soak in hot water for 45 minutes under cover. Put the chiles and the water they soaked in in a blender with the garlic and puree. Stir in the oil and pulque. Season with salt and add the chiles and onion.

4 ounces *pasilla* chiles
6 pickled *serrano* chiles
2 cloves garlic
3 tablespoons olive oil
2 cups of pulque or light beer
Salt to taste
2 onions, finely chopped

FISH SAUCE

Salsa para Pescado

Fry the onions in olive oil until golden. Add the tomatoes and chiles and sauté 3 minutes longer. Add water, parsley, oregano, salt, and pepper and cook 10 more minutes. Add sherry and chopped olives and remove from heat.

2 large onions, chopped
3 tablespoons olive oil
2 large tomatoes, chopped
2 green chiles, seeded and chopped
¼ cup hot water
3 sprigs parsley, chopped
½ teaspoon oregano
1 teaspoon salt
½ teaspoon pepper
⅓ cup dry sherry
15 pitted olives, chopped

GREEN SAUCE

Salsa Verde

Quarter the tomatoes and put in a blender with the other ingredients. Blend to a coarse puree. Serve as an accompaniment to everything but dessert.

6 Mexican green tomatoes, with parchment skin removed (or 1 10-ounce can green tomatoes, drained)
1 medium onion, roughly chopped
2 fresh or canned green chiles
1 large clove garlic
3 sprigs fresh coriander, or ¼ teaspoon ground
1 teaspoon salt

GUACAMOLE

Peel avocados and chop in small pieces. Mix together with the onion, tomatoes, chiles, and coriander.

To preserve the color of the avocado:
1. Bury the pits in the guacamole;
2. Do not add salt until just before serving;
3. Cover tightly and refrigerate until needed.

If you take these precautions the guacamole should not discolor for many hours.

3 medium avocados, not too ripe
1 medium onion, chopped
2 medium tomatoes, peeled, and chopped
2 green chiles, or canned *serrano* or *jalapeño* chiles, finely chopped
2 tablespoons chopped fresh coriander, or a pinch of ground coriander
Salt and pepper to taste

MEXICAN SAUCE

Salsa Mexicana

Mix all ingredients and let set for ½ hour before serving. There is no possibility that a dish has been invented over the past 8000 years, beyond dessert, which Salsa Mexicana does not complement. It may be the greatest all-purpose sauce in history.

1 large onion, chopped
1 pound tomatoes, peeled and finely chopped
3 *serrano* chiles, chopped
2 sprigs fresh coriander or parsley, chopped
1 teaspoon salt
1 large clove garlic, finely chopped

PUMPKIN-SEED SAUCE

Salsa Pipián

Fry or toast the seeds, garlic, and bread in hot lard. Drain on paper towels, reserving the skillet with the lard. Grind these fried ingredients in a blender as finely as possible. Prepare the chiles and cover with as much of the 3 cups water as necessary. Put ground ingredients together in the reserved skillet and simmer slowly, adding the flour, the remaining water, and the honey. Cook until thick, stirring constantly.

Pipián is a sauce for all fowl and poultry.

1 cup squash or pumpkin seeds
½ cup sesame seeds
2 cloves garlic
3 slices toasted French bread
3 tablespoons lard
4 *ancho* chiles
3 cups water
1 tablespoon flour
3 teaspoons honey

DESSERTS *DULCES Y POSTRES*

BREAD PUDDING EVALINA
Capirotada Evalina

CHOCOLATE PUDDING TO THE TASTE OF GEORGE THE SAILOR
Budín de Chocolate al Gusto de Jorge el Marinero

CHONGOS ZAMORANOS

COCONUT CUSTARD HEATHER
Cocada Brezo

DATE AND NUT CAKE FAVORED BY THE SAN ANTONIO BANKER
Torta de Dátiles y Nueces del Banquero de San Antonio

GLAMOUR DE MANGO CHANTILLY IN THE STYLE OF DEBBIE
Glamor de Mango Chantilly Estilo Debbie

MACEDONIA

MISS JUPP'S NUTTY BANANA CAKE
Torta de Nueces y Plátanos de la Señorita Jupp

NITO SWEET AND NUTTY
Dulce de Nueces Nito

LAZY BONES
Flojeras

BREAD PUDDING EVALINA

Capirotada Evalina

Cut the toast into quarters and fry in butter and oil, using 3 tablespoons at a time for 8 or 10 quarters of bread. Boil together brown sugar and ½ cup water with aniseed, cinnamon, and cloves, until this becomes a thick syrup. In a buttered baking dish make a layer of fried bread squares, a layer of cheese, then raisins and pine nuts, and pour over this some of the syrup. Make another similar layer and, if your dish is small and deep, then consecutive layers until all the ingredients are used. Sprinkle ⅓ cup water as evenly as possible over all and bake, covered, in a moderate oven for 18 minutes.
Serves 6.

10 slices bread, toasted
1 stick butter (¼ pound), melted
¼ cup olive oil
1 cup brown sugar
½ cup water
½ teaspoon aniseed
1 teaspoon ground cinnamon
½ teaspoon whole cloves
1 cup thinly sliced Monterey Jack cheese
½ cup raisins
½ cup pine nuts
⅓ cup water

CHOCOLATE PUDDING TO THE TASTE OF GEORGE THE SAILOR

Budín de Chocolate al Gusto de Jorge el Marinero

When the cream is partially stiff, add the sugar, salt, beaten egg yolks, chocolate, cinnamon, and vanilla extract, and whip until thoroughly blended. Spoon into 6 individual serving dishes or glasses and top with chopped pecans (but just before serving so they won't get soggy). Chill until ready to serve. Serves 6.

1 pint whipping cream
1 cup powdered sugar
½ teaspoon salt
4 egg yolks, well beaten
2 ounces semisweet chocolate, finely grated
½ teaspoon ground cinnamon
1 teaspoon vanilla extract
½ cup pecans, very finely chopped

CHONGOS ZAMORANOS

It is important to use neither hot nor cold milk, but always lukewarm; do not boil. Measure the milk into a fireproof deep dish. Beat the egg yolks, then add to lukewarm milk. Dissolve a rennet tablet in a little water, then add to the egg and milk, stirring gently for as little a time as possible. Place the mixture in a warm place to permit the rennet to set firmly. Cut deeply into firm rennet to make scorings in which to sprinkle the sugar and bits of cinnamon stick (or sugar previously mixed with the powdered cinnamon). Using an asbestos mat or a Pyrex guard, place over low heat and cook until the sugar has formed a thick syrup. Allow about 2 hours to cook.

2 quarts milk (not previously boiled)
4 egg yolks
1 rennet tablet
2 cups sugar
1 stick cinnamon

DATE AND NUT CAKE FAVORED BY THE SAN ANTONIO BANKER

Torta de Dátiles y Nueces del Banquero de San Antonio

Stir baking powder into flour. Add the dates and the nuts. Beat the eggs until frothy and stir these plus the sugar and the orange juice into the flour mixture. Beat until well blended. Spread on an 8×10-inch greased baking dish and bake in moderate oven for ½ hour. Serve with light cream. Serves 8.

2 teaspoons baking powder
½ cup flour
1 pound dates, pitted and sliced
1 cup pecans broken into small pieces
4 eggs
1 cup sugar
¼ cup orange juice
Light cream

COCONUT CUSTARD HEATHER

Cocada Brezo

Boil the sugar, water, and cinnamon together for 10 minutes. Remove the cinnamon and add the coconut. Cook this over low heat or until the coconut has absorbed all the syrup—about 20 minutes. Be sure to stir often. Meanwhile, warm the milk and, when the coconut is dry, add the milk. Stirring constantly, cook slowly until the mixture has thickened. Put ¼ cup of coconut mixture into the beaten eggs and mix well. Add eggs and sherry to pudding and continue cooking slowly, stirring constantly, until thick. Pour into a serving dish and, when cool, sprinkle with almonds and refrigerate.
Serves 6–8.

1 cup sugar
1 cup water
2 large cinnamon sticks
4 ounces shredded coconut
4 cups milk
3 egg yolks, well beaten
¼ cup sherry
Toasted almonds

GLAMOUR DE MANGO CHANTILLY IN THE STYLE OF DEBBIE

Glamor de Mango Chantilly Estilo Debbie

Peel and crush the mangoes. Whip in the powdered sugar. Whip the cream with 1 teaspoon sugar until stiff. Chop the oranges finely. Fold in the whipped cream and pecans. Pour into individual serving dishes and chill.
Serves 8.

4 fresh or canned mangoes
¾ cup + 1 teaspoon powdered sugar
1 pint whipping cream
2 oranges
1 cup pecans broken into small pieces

MACEDONIA

Peel the orange and chop it into small pieces. Slice the bananas and drop them in lemon juice for a few seconds. Chop the pineapple into small pieces. Mix the strawberries, pineapple, ¾ cup sugar, and white wine. Whip the cream with 1 teaspoon sugar. Add the orange and bananas to the other fruit. Fold in the whipped cream. Chill in individual dessert dishes.
Serves 6.

1 orange
2 bananas
Juice of 1 lemon
2 1-inch pineapple slices
1½ cups fresh strawberries
¾ cup + 1 teaspoon powdered sugar
¼ cup dry white wine
1 pint whipping cream

MISS JUPP'S NUTTY BANANA CAKE

Torta de Nueces y Plátanos de la Señorita Jupp

Boil the sugar and water until it becomes syrup. Remove from heat. Cream the butter and beaten eggs together. Add this to the still-warm syrup. Slice 2½ bananas into the bottom of a buttered baking dish. Sprinkle half the chopped pecans over the bananas. Spoon syrup over the pecans. Slice another 2½ bananas and cover these with the remaining pecans. Spoon syrup over this layer. Slice remaining 3 bananas over this and cover the top of the dish with all the walnuts. Pour the remaining syrup over the dessert and bake in a moderate oven for 10 minutes. Serves 6.

½ cup sugar
½ cup water
⅓ cup butter
2 eggs, beaten
8 bananas
¾ cup chopped pecans
1 cup finely chopped walnuts

NITO SWEET AND NUTTY

Dulce de Nueces Nito

Boil the sugar and water, stirring occasionally. Cook until it registers at the soft-ball mark on a candy thermometer or until it forms a soft ball when dropped in cold water. Mix the nuts thoroughly with the milk. Add to this the beaten egg yolks. Using an egg beater or a whisk, beat this mixture well. Add to the boiling syrup and stir continuously over low heat until thick. Remove from heat and beat for 3 minutes. Pour into large or individual serving dish and cool. Serve with whipped cream. Whip the cream with a teaspoon of powdered sugar; when nearly stiff, add the Kahlúa and beat another minute. Serves 8.

1 pound powdered sugar
1 cup water
1 pound walnuts, crushed into tiny pieces
1 cup milk
5 egg yolks, beaten
1 pint whipping cream
4 tablespoons Kahlúa (coffee liqueur)

LAZY BONES

Flojeras

If pitted prunes are not available, use regular prunes and pit them yourself when cooked, being careful not to tear the prunes. Squeeze the orange, reserve the juice, and grate the rind. Cook the prunes with honey, water, juice, and rind until tender—about 20 minutes. Whip the cream with sugar and add pecans. Drain the prunes, reserving the liquid. With your

½ pound large prunes, pitted
1 orange
1 cup honey
1 cup water
¼ cup whipping cream
1 teaspoon sugar
2 tablespoons finely chopped pecans
2 egg yolks
1 tablespoon cornstarch
½ cup milk
½ cup light cream
½ teaspoon salt

thumbs, round out ample interior space in each prune. Fill centers of prunes with whipped cream. Beat the egg yolks together with the cornstarch. Combine with the liquid in which the prunes cooked and add the milk, light cream, and salt. Cook, stirring, over low heat until thickened. Cool, then beat well. Pour into serving dish and chill. Just before serving, spoon the prunes into the custard.
Serves 8.

SUGGESTED MENUS

Five Breakfast/Brunch Menus

Four Lunch Menus

Four Dinner Menus

FIVE BREAKFAST/BRUNCH MENUS

Tortilla Soup
Avocado Stuffed with Shrimp, Garnished with Tostads

Huevos Rancheros
Frijoles Refritos
Salsa Mexicana

Ceviche
Tostadas Compuestas with Hot Sauce

Sopa Sencilla
Chilaquiles con Pollo
Frijoles Refritos

Papatzul
Ensalada Pesadumbre
Mango Ice Cream

FOUR LUNCH MENUS

Crepas con Pollo en Salsa Verde
Macedonia

Arroz con Camarones
Ensalada de Calabacitas y Aguacate
Flojeras

Pozole
Totopos con Guacamole

Torta Azteca
Crown of Rice
Budín de Chocolate

FOUR DINNER MENUS

Sopa de Zanahoria
Lomo Desmond Guinness
Chiles en Nogada
Capirotada

Sopa de Camote
Pipián Verde de Camarones
Arroz Blanco
Ensalada de Nochebuena
Dulce de Nuez

Sopa de Elote
Pollo Tabasqueño
Lentejas con Puerco
Cocada Brezo

Sopa de Frijol
Albóndigas
Coliflor Estilo Puebla
Ensalada de Aguacate
Glamor de Mango Chantilly

SOURCES OF SUPPLY
FUENTES DE PROVISIÓN

The components of the foregoing recipes can be found in Mexican, Spanish, Puerto Rican, Chinese, Indian, and Italian food shops in your town or city.

Write to the nearest Mexican consul, enclosing a stamped, self-addressed envelope, asking him where he buys his ingredients for Mexican food.

Fancy food shops often carry a variety of canned Mexican food ingredients. If they don't carry these in stock, they will order them for you.

ALL HERBS AND SPICES
Mail Order:
> Kalustyan Orient Expert Trading Corp. 123 Lexington Avenue, New York, N.Y. 10016
> Seems to carry every known aromatic in the world. Free brochure.

Mail Order and Direct:
> Mr. Jesus Moneo
> Casa Moneo
> 218 West Fourteenth Street, New York, N.Y. 10011
> Most complete shopping for all-around Latin American food of all kinds.

FANCY FOOD STORES (Mail Order and Direct)
East:
> Casa Moneo
> 218 West Fourteenth Street
> New York, New York 10011

> B. Altman & Co.
> Fifth Avenue at Thirty-fourth Street
> New York, New York 10016

> Bloomingdale's Delicacies Shop
> Lexington Avenue at Fifty-ninth Street
> New York, New York 10022

> La Sevillana
> 2469 Eighteenth Street N.W.
> Washington, D.C. 20009

> The Fancy Food Shop
> John Wanamaker
> Philadelphia, Pennsylvania

> The Valley Food Mart
> 6241 Falls Road
> Baltimore, Maryland 21209

South:
> Barrett & Leach
> 3771 Roswell Road N.W.
> Atlanta, Georgia 30342

> J. Goldsmith & Sons
> 123 South Main Street
> Memphis, Tennessee 38103

> The Simon David Grocery
> 7117 Inwood Road
> Dallas, Texas 75209

> Hunt's Grocery
> 4527 Maple Street
> Dallas, Texas 75219

Antone's Import Company
807 Taft Street *and*
8111 Main at Old Spanish Trail
Houston, Texas 77025

Pizzini's
202 Produce Row
San Antonio, Texas 78207

The Fancy Food Shop   Joske Brothers
Alamo Plaza
San Antonio, Texas 78205

Antone's Import Company
2606 South Sheridan
Tulsa, Oklahoma 74129

Southeast:

The Fancy Food Shop
The Jordan Marsh Company
  (many branches)
Miami, Florida

Bustani's
354 South County Road
Palm Beach, Florida 33480

Middle West:

Casa Esteiro
2719 West Division
Chicago, Illinois 60622

The Fancy Food Shop   Younker Brothers
Seventh and Walnut
Des Moines, Iowa 52802

Donaldson's
601 Nicollet Avenue
Minneapolis, Minnesota 55402

The Wolferman Store
Kansas City, Missouri

The Fancy Food Shops of the Famous Barr Store
  (many branches)
St. Louis, Missouri

Roffman's House of Delicacies
2500 Harney Street
Omaha, Nebraska 68131

West:

La Luz del Día
610 North Spring Street
Los Angeles, California 90012

The Fancy Food Shop
The Albert T. Balzer Company
Los Angeles, California

Le Gourmet Shop
Pine Inn
Carmel, California 93921

The Fancy Pantry
7852 Girard Street
La Jolla, California 92037

The Fancy Food Shop
The Auerbach Company
Salt Lake City, Utah

The Fremont Grocery
616 Central Avenue S.W.
Albuquerque, New Mexico 87101

Kitchen Equipment (Direct and Mail Order):
For earthenware casseroles and baking dishes, *molinillos, molcajetes,* etc.

Casa Moneo
218 West Fourteenth Street
New York, New York 10011

Fresh Tortillas and Ready Mexican Food (New York Only):
Mexi-Frost Specialties Co., Inc.
220 West Thirteenth Street
New York, New York 10011

Fresh, warm tortillas and tamales and empanadas cannot be sent by mail. The shop will deliver for a minimum order, but it's fun to pick them up yourself to see this immaculate shop.

Tortillas, made fresh daily, can be picked up after noon from:

Xochitl
146 West Forty-sixth Street,
New York, New York 10036

GLOSSARY *GLOSARIO* OF MEXICAN FOOD TERMS

ACEITE: Cooking oil. Since one of the legs of the tripod of Mexican cooking is corn, let this cooking oil be corn oil. However, peanuts originated in Mexico. Spain, Mexico's "discoverer," is one of the producers of fine olives so, in that order, the other two oils will do. Think of Pliny's wisdom as you cook with it: "It is not with oil as with wine; for by age it acquires a bad flavor and at the end of the year it is already old. This is a wise provision of nature. Wine, which tends to drunkenness, she invites us to keep; but she has not willed that we should be thus sparing of oil, so has rendered its use common and universal by the very necessity of using it while fresh."

ACEITUNA: The olive of all antiquity and now; the first fruit of the Mediterranean; the messenger of ancient Greece.

ACHIOTE: A powdered food coloring from the waxy coating of the annatto fruit.

ADOBADO: Thin sheets of marinated beef or pork which have been dried.

ADOBO: Seasonings rubbed on meat before cooking or drying.

AGAVE: The century plant, which is cultivated in five species for the manufacture of pulque, tequila, and mescal: each alcoholic. The *agave* leaves are also used for fiber, and as roofing for small houses. The plant produced the soap and the writing paper of the Aztecs. In defiance of the alleged "*mañana* syndrome" of Mexico, the century plant, which can take 80 to 90 years to blossom elsewhere, blooms every 9 to 12 years in the republic.

AGUACATE: The avocado, called *ahuacatl* by the Aztecs, provided the "butter" of cowless ancient Mexico in the form of guacamole, which is used as a spread, with meat, in soup, and as salad.

AL HORNO: Baked or roasted, which, traditionally in Mexico, is always done without a cover. Eneas Sweetland Dallas, first and last of the scholar-journalists, he who wrote an 8½-column obituary of Lord Palmerston in the *Times* of London in 1865, said: "The chemist who will tell us the precise difference between baking and roasting will confer a benefit on mankind. We all see, or fancy that we see, a difference in the results, but what it is no one has been able to define." The best results in Mexican cuisine are obtained by cooking in earthenware vessels because earthenware is such a poor heat conductor that it takes a longer time to build heat with them and a longer time for them to cool—the ideal condition for putting the most flavor into soups and casseroles.

ALBÓNDIGAS EN CHILE: Balls of ground meat and eggs in chile.

ALCACHOFA: The artichoke. A somewhat disaffected fellow once wrote: "It is good for a man to eat thistles, to remember that he is an ass." The artichoke is the best of thistles and the vegetable which produces the most waste while yielding the least used. If served with spareribs the dish could be the ritual food of the consumer society. The enormous trouble that must be taken to cook artichokes and their bottoms made Victor Hugo say, "It is as if the Deity were to bombard a lettuce with a thunderbolt."

ALCAPARRA: The caper. The friend of sauces, the hyssop of the Good Book, "which springeth out of the wall."

AJO: Garlic. The blessing upon us all. It is a member of the lily family (*Allium sativum*). In Numbers XI:5, the Israelites cry out to Moses, in despair, for garlic. Fifteen pounds of it could buy a healthy Egyptian slave. The fastidious ancient Greeks seldom used it in their cooking, but the Romans chewed up dazzling amounts of garlic because they considered it to be aphrodisiac. How else to ward off vampires except with the blessed bulb? Pliny listed 61 diseases garlic was supposed to cure. Modern doctors take this half seriously because garlic forces people to keep their distance, lessening the possibilities of contagion. Experiments published in the *Journal of the American Medical Association* show that garlic packs such an olfactory wallop because, unlike other foods whose odors merely cling to teeth and tongue, the garlic oils enter the lungs to be exhaled with every breath and through every pore. At the moment Henri IV of France was born his gums were rubbed with garlic, but Don Quixote forbade it to Sancho Panza as being unseemly in the Governor of Barataria. Garlic is universally used in Mexican food. The finest and most sophisticated garlic is produced by the Brenner method in the "hot" soil of the state of Aguascalientes. That garlic is an efficacious food for the tropics is described in Monteire's *Angola and the River Congo* (Vol. II, p. 240): "Garlic I consider the most valuable article of food in a hot climate, especially when eaten raw. I never traveled without a supply of garlic, and I found its beneficial effects on the stomach and system most marked. It produces a delightful sensation of repose." Garlic is obtainable in every possible dehydrated state: powdered, instant, ground, minced, chopped, sliced, or pureed, but there is little excuse for using them when fresh garlic, if not the great Brenner garlic, is available everywhere.

AJONJOLÍ: Sesame. An oily seed used in baking, desserts, and sauces or toasted for use as a garnish. Italian cooks have greatly refined the use of sesame, but its uses are as superstitious as they are tasty, going back 400 years to what the herbalists had developed as "the Doctrine of Signatures" in which every plant was seen to have an appearance or activities which identified their meanings. Sesame seeds pop and scatter away from their plant as soon as they are ripe, so sesame was called the seed which could free itself of all barriers. Scheherazade had Ali Baba shout "Open Sesame!" to enter the robbers' cave. Sesame is not only among the most ancient of spices but is also high in protein.

ALHABAR: Basil, or sweet basil. A plant of the labiate family which abounds in potherbs (mint, marjoram, savory, and others). Its leaves have a strong flavor of cloves, are used in salads as well as in the pot. Basil delivers the signal of springtime in the greatest of all pasta sauces: *al pesto*, second only to guacamole in its evocation of eternal *primavera*. In Italy and in Rumania, basil has uses beyond the kitchen. Any Italian girl who wears a sprig of basil is suggesting that there is no need for young men to keep their distance. If a Rumanian accepts basil from a woman, and wears it in his buttonhole, he is engaged.

ALMENDRA: Almond. The most versatile and useful of nuts. Its shape conjures up the eyes of houris and geishas, then its content startles, when we know that it yields the most potent and rapid of poisons: hydrocyanic acid, or cyanide, and prussic acid. The almond actually blossoms before its leaves come out; it is a peach and a nectarine at the same time, being the parent of both. As with human families, the same almond tree can produce both sweet and bitter almonds. It favors children and fatties with nougats and macaroons, sugared almonds, and pralines. It provides an admirable salve for the skin. A few almonds eaten after dinner give instant relief from heartburn. Almond milk has many of the characteristics of animal milk: a soothing beverage, a refreshing summer drink. Almonds are the per-fumer's treasure, and what remains after the oil has been extracted once made a face powder called *pâte d'amandes*. The husks are so rich in alkalines that they turn into soap.

ANCHOA: Anchovy. The most renowned herring in the world, the foundation of the celebrated sauces of classical times—garum and alec—and the ancient Indo-Chinese *muoc-mam*. Dr. Charles Badham, the English physician, versifier, and translator of Juvenal's *Satires*, wrote that the anchovy "was to the ancient world what the herring is to the modern and furnishing the materials for the finest fish sauce either on record or in use." Anchovies appeal to Mexican cooks as a flavoring rather than as an ingredient. Anchovies are excellent with sauces and they marry with eggs.

ANÍS: Anise. The hard-working brother of the family which includes carraway, cumin, dill, and coriander. Even more than the others, anise possesses a carminative virtue and is therefore much prized by cuisines which tend to produce flatulence. It has other uses far afield. On the Kilmoganny pampas region of County Kilkenny, Ireland, aniseed is used to simulate the odor of a fox. To make the most of a very good run, the huntsman goes forth in the morning, dragging after him a bag of aniseed, choosing the best line across country for an exhilarating and not-too-easy ride. The hounds always follow this scent as a genuine fox, to the finish. The method is called Hunt's Hunt after Lady Evelyn, the humanitarian mistress of Rossenarra.

ANTOJITO: The diminutive of *antojo*, i.e., a whim or capricious desire. *Antojitos* are believed by the citizens of the Colossus of the North to be the entire cuisine of Mexico (excepting *chile con carne*). Eating *antojitos* such as tacos, *garnachas, charupas, quesadillas, tostadas,* and so on is more habit-forming than trampoline jumping. These eternal delights which transform everyone's appetite into a gastronomic compulsion of nocturnal pickle eaters in pregnancy were in no way the inventions of John Montagu, Earl of Sandwich, but rather the 6000-year-old forerunners of all the carbohydrate-enclosed, hand-held food in the world—the point of origin of all sandwiches in history. Including the invention of the calendar, the symbol for zero, the rules for basketball and *mole negro*, the *antojito* is Mexico's greatest contribution to world civilization.

APIO: Celery.

ARROZ: Rice. The national food of India, Southeast Asia, China, and Japan, the staple of more than half of the world's population (which gets 80 percent of all its calories from rice); contains as much nourishment as the potato and is digested in an hour. Rice is highest and most varied among the one-dish meals of the world: In Japan, *asa gohan, hiru gohan,* and *yoru gohan* (meaning morning rice, afternoon rice, and evening rice to describe the 3 main meals of the day); the paella of Spain, the Arabian pilaf, and the Indian pilau, the American Creole jambalaya, Italian risotto and *risi e bisi,* Indonesian rijsttafel and *arroz mexicano*. Long-grain rice is to be used for all of these except risotto, in which the short-grained is used because the cooked rice should have more the consistency of a pudding. Rice is the Chinese and Hindu symbol of fertility, which is why newlyweds are showered with it. The Mexican caution for judging the amount of raw rice for the number of diners: ¼ cup for each lady, ½ cup for each man. Rice, one of the oldest cultivated crops in the world, originated in southern India. The Arabs took it to Spain. The Spanish brought it to Mexico.

ASADO: Roasted (meat).

ASAR: To roast something quickly, generally over an open flame, as with chiles, peppers, and tomatoes.

AZAFRÁN: Saffron. The most expensive aromatic because it takes 96,000 *Crocus sativus* stigmas to make a single pound. Saffron is a spice, a food coloring, a cosmetic, a fabric dye, and a medicine. It is perhaps one of the few food products best purchased at your friendly, neighborhood drugstore. Don't use saffron lavishly. Think of how few strands of it were needed to make Homer's "saffron-robed morning."

AZÚCAR: Sugar. It is not too clearly taught that sugar plays an important part in all food. There must be sugar in all soups and sauces. What are carrots, turnips, parsnips, onions, celery, and the rest but repositories of delicately flavored sugars? The sophisticated sugar content of all local food is why the wine of every region marries best with the food the region cooks. A classical, very dry red wine drunk with a carrot-happy Scotch broth, dredged with onions, tastes like a bad idea. Further, the cook who works with natural sugar from vegetables must calculate whether they make the food sufficiently sweet and, if he thinks not, adds sugar. The principal supply of sugar in continental Europe and in those exotic islands immediately west of Holland comes from the beet, whose crystals were first obtained by the German chemist Andreas Margraf in the eighteenth century. Mexican sugar is cane sugar of the sort which Cortés' captains described as "reeds which make honey without bees." Sugar cane was grown by ancient Polynesians and in prehistoric India.

BACALAO: Cod. Mexicans eat a lot of cod, and the cod eats more fish than any other of its size. It is estimated that the cod catch for Mexico eats as much herring as the entire herring-hung population of the British Isles and the Republic of Ireland combined. Cod can digest crabs, and have been caught with as many as forty-two crabs *in situ*. Cod have taken other fishes' places on a hook by eating the fish on the hook, then the hook. Its gastric juices are so potent that it turns lobsters engulfed in it as bright red as does a pot of boiling water. The cod is the winnowing goat of the sea. Not only is it a fish which can digest almost anything, it is the most digestible. Cheater cheated, eater eaten. *C'est la vie.*

BARBACOA MEXICANA: Pit barbecue—that is Bar-B-Q—of mutton or goat. Can produce salivation with the force of a power hose among *barbacoa* adepts. Ah, love, a quire of warm tortillas, a *barbacoa mexicana,* and thou beside me burping in the wilderness.

BATIR: Beat in, whip in, or fold in.

BECERRO: Calf, which is what most of the fighting bulls of Mexico seem to be to Spaniards.

BERENJENA: Eggplant.

BETABEL: Red beet; also called *remolacha.*

BOLILLO: Hard roll.

CABRITO ASADO: Broiled young kid, a startling tactile-texture change for eaters of taller, older meat. Pussycat meat may have this consistency and give.

CACAHUATE: Peanut. Called *tlalcáhuatl* in Mexico before the Conquest, meaning earth chocolate. The nut, a true pea, originated in Mexico, has high protein and iron value, is an important application to sauces, garnishes, and three-ring circuses, and is one of the world's most valuable sources of oil for cooking and the manufacture of margarine. When the oil is extracted the remaining peanut is used as animal feed. Query: Is the Charles Schulz cartoon strip called Cacahuates in Mexico?

CAL: Lime. Oxide of calcium, which is used in cooking corn kernels for making the flour which becomes tortillas, which, because of the *cal* content, give Mexicans strong, white teeth.

CALABAZA: Squash, pumpkin, or gourd. A Spanish word

which is probably oriental in origin in that the Persian word for watermelon is *kharbuza*. The varieties of *calabazas* are far more numerous than Adler's one-armed bobsled drivers and rove on from baby zucchini through Turk's turban to giant pumpkins pulled by chic mice. Pumpkin seeds are the mainstay of a distinguished, staple Mexican sauce called *pipián*. Everything from the great soups to breads and pies is made from *calabazas*, and you jes' know that includes stews, because their outstanding quality is being able to absorb and retain the flavor of whatever they are cooked with while imparting a natural sweetness.

CALABAZA DE TACHA: Pumpkin baked with brown sugar.

CAJETE: A thick, sweet sauce from Celeya, used as a spread.

CALDO: Broth or stock. The word is also used for a rich soup of meat and vegetables.

CAMOTE: Sweet potato.

CAMARÓN: Shrimp, for which the Chinese word is *ha*, surely an expression of approval. Shrimp (Chinese plural: *ha-ha*) is so popular all over the world that it was the cause of the world's first international trade association to facilitate its distribution. However, until the end of the nineteenth century, the bulk of the shrimp catch was used as bait for commercial fishermen and the rest turned into fertilizer. Shrimp range in size from ten to twelve "jumbos" to sixty tiny Alaskan shrimp per pound. The sweetest-tasting shrimp, that which is used in Mexican cooking, runs to about twenty-five to a pound. Shrimp, no matter what the size, should not be cooked for longer than five minutes, in salted water, then chilled in a covered vessel, preferably directly upon ice cubes.

CANELA: Cinnamon. Perhaps the oldest known spice in the world. It comes from the bark of a species of laurel from whose root is extracted a juice which hardens into camphor. It is not to be confused with cassia, which is called Chinese cinnamon and is in great request in Turkey, Russia, the United States, and Germany because it is coarser and stronger—but hardly the real thing. Cassia is rich, reddish-brown. True cinnamon is bright, light-brown, almost yellowish—its flavor is sweet and delicate. It makes a helluvan ice cream flavor.

CANGREJO: Crab, but generally called *jaiba* in Mexico.

CARNE: Meat. Outside the kitchen this is a term used to plead with overzealous bullfighters who are determined to try for one more linked pass. And the customer is, in this instance, almost always right.

CARNE ASADA: Broiled fillet of beef.

CARNE DE RES: Beef.

CARNERO: Mutton, which always seems to be called lamb everywhere. I asked for it in London one time and the butcher said, "We haven't carried mutton in *years*. Just no call for it." Mutton is the meat of a mature sheep, usually between a year and eighteen months but—since lamb may not be older than six months—how does one cook the hiatus?

CASTAÑAS: Chestnuts.

CEBADA: Barley. It was grown in Switzerland during the Stone Age and, across time, has actually been phased out by wheat because barley has less protein. Barley is used to brew beer and if beer had more protein it would be less fattening, but have you ever tried wheaten beer?

CEBOLLA: Onion is an onion is an onion is not a leek, scallion, garlic bulb, or shallot. After salt the onion is the most valuable of all flavoring ingredients, causing people who detest onions and are vocal about it to eat approximately 218 pounds of onions for each ten years of their lives. The onion is a member of the lily family and is said to have originated in the Hindu Kush, which are such high, cold mountains that the first onions would be very strong and very small because the rule is: The warmer the climate, the larger the onion and the milder its flavor. Onions are white, yellow, and purple-red.

CEVICHE: Pickled raw seafood in chiles and tomato sauce with *limón.*

CENA: Supper, traditionally a "light" meal in Mexico

CHAYOTE: Christophine. A large, pear-shaped fruit with one seed. About five to eight inches long, chayote is a very special squash which grows with some ninety-nine other chayotes on vines fifty to seventy feet long. It is as old as the Mayas. Chayote fanciers are wildly fond of what they like.

CHICHA: Sugar-cane brandy, a favorite in the state of Chiapas and in the high Andes, which are a fur piece to the south.

CHICHARRONES: Mexican pork crackling made by rendering the lard from the fat under the pork skin and cooking it until golden brown.

CHILE: The spices of life, love, and the pursuit of ultimate nourishment in the most memorable way; the reason why Hernán Cortés lingered in Mexico for ten years after the Conquest, despite his unpopularity.

CHILE POBLANO: A large, sweet, green chile which is stuffed: i.e., *Chiles Rellenos en Nogada,* stuffed green pepper with walnut and pomegranate-seed sauce. In the United States substitute a green bell pepper.

CHILAQUILES: Stale tortillas fried, then cooked in a hot chile and tomato sauce.

CHAMPIÑON: Mushroom.

CHIRIMOYA: Mexican fruit related to the custard apple. It is eaten raw, sprinkled with cinnamon and, sometimes, lime juice. It tastes like all twenty-eight flavors of Señor Howard Johnson's ice cream.

CHOCOLATE: Chocolate, or *xocolatl,* Aztec for sour water, a favorite drink of Moctezuma, flavored with honey and cinnamon and whipped to a froth. For centuries seafaring men have considered chocolate second only to rum as a restorative—with which it has a fine affinity when used together in cooking. Tarahumara Indian runners who keep going for days and nights subsist while running on pellets of chocolate, perhaps augmented with peyote. Chocolate is an important ingredient of Mexico's ancient imperial sauce: *mole.*

CHONGOS: A traditional Mexican dessert; a junket hardened with sweet syrup. All *chongos* are delicious, but the greatest of these are the *chongos zamoranos* of the state of Michoacán. *Chongos* means "little knots."

CHÍCHARO: The round, green pea.

CILANTRO: Coriander, also called Chinese parsley. It is a staple of Indian and southern Chinese as well as Mexican cooking. The seeds are tiny and yellowish and give a warm to hot flavor which is between sage and lemon peel. Cilantro is also used commercially to help gin, and to flavor sausages and wild game to help people over the gin.

CLAVO DE ESPECIA: Clove. Sounds prettiest in French: *clou de girofle*, nail of the caryophyllum. However, a clove of garlic does not mean a nail, it means something cloven. Clove is the thirstiest of spices and its unexpanded flowers will increase their weight if water is placed near them, greatly aiding dealers with honest scales. The clove, of the myrtle family, is a tree which grows as tall and thick as a man's body; the fragrant cloves grow at twig-end, ten or twenty in a cluster. They grow only at higher altitudes. Madagascar is now the clove supplier to the world.

COCER: To boil and, generally, to cook.

COCHINITO: Suckling pig.

COCO: Coconut, commonly called *rallado* in Mexico. It is the fruit of the coconut palm tree. Cocada, a concentrated candy, is one by-product.

COL: Cabbage, also called *repollo*. There are over a hundred varieties of *Brassica oleracea*. Cabbage is related to Brussels sprouts, cauliflower, broccoli, kohlrabi, spring greens, and turnips. The Emperor Tiberius believed cabbage prevented drunkenness and, considering his life-style, he probably smoked it. Mexicans are fond of a Chinese cabbage called *pets'ai* which looks like a large romaine or cos lettuce with almost white leaves and crisp stalks which give out very little odor while cooking.

COLAR: To strain or sieve.

COMIDA: Dinner, the Mexican midday meal, the main meal of the day.

COMINO: Cumin, a member of the parsley family which is essential to all Indian curries and to all commercial curry and chile powders. It is stronger than carraway but greatly like it in shape, taste, and aroma.

CUAJAR: To curdle.

DÁTIL: Date; the fruit of the date palm.

DESAYUNO: Breakfast; by tradition, not a light meal.

DESHEBRAR: To shred.

DESLEÍR: To thin or dissolve in liquid.

DULCE DE NUEZ: A walnut confection.

DURAZNO: Peach. In English, peach is a corruption of the Latin word for Persia, *amygdalus Persica* or *Persica vulgaris*. Almonds, nectarines, and peaches may be found growing on the same tree, even on the same branch. The fruit itself is sometimes a peach on one side, a nectarine on the other. Both are divided into two varieties: Freestone and Clingstone. The former are better, the peaches for dessert. Clingstones are for stewing. There are over two thousand varieties of peaches, the first of which were cultivated in China two thousand years ago, then spread westward over the caravan routes to the Mediterranean. By 1600 it was a staple in Mexico.

EJOTE: The string bean.

ELOTE: Corn on the cob.

EMPANAR: To bread.

ENELDO: Dill. Marvelous with sauces, green beans, cucumbers, potato salad, sauerkraut, and macaroni and cheese; but, more importantly, to witches and the cursed alike, it is *the* binding ingredient in magic and countermagic potions. For example: there is nothing like dill to ward off the evil eye. To the chosen few million who have wandered into Jewish delicatessens in the city of New York, dill is alive and well and living in sour pickles.

ENCHILADAS: A prime *antojito*.

ENHARINAR: To roll in flour for frying.

ENJUAGAR: To rinse.

EN NOGADA: With nuts.

A LA PARRILLA: Grilled.

ENTREMESES: Hors d'oeuvres.

EPAZOTE: An aromatic herb essential to the cooking of Mexican beans, the foundation stone of a Mexican breakfast.

ESCABECHE: A pickling marinade. Sauerbraten is not just a word but a way of life across the world no matter what the Tahitians or the Mexicans call it.

ESPARRAGO: Asparagus, the near-of-kin to lily of the valley. Because of a twinship with asphodels it is said that the fields of Elysium are paved with asparagus, but he who said that is out to lunch and we cannot check it now. The French, involved with the Champs-Élysées, still retain asparagus root in their pharmacopoeia to sooth the action of the heart, to have rapid action on the kidneys. No matter what the diner beside you is doing, asparagus should be eaten with the fingers.

ESPESAR: To thicken.

ESTILAR: To drain.

ESTOFADO: A meat and vegetable stew.

ESTOFAR: To stew.

FIDEOS: Noodles. Even in English we never speak of Italians eating noodles because Italians have far more serious names for their two hundred and seventeen varieties. *Fideos,* a Mexican word, should really have been the Italian word for noodles, instead of tagliarini or fettucine, because, as the noodle has been faithful to Italians, so have Italians been faithful to the noodle.

FREÍR: To fry. If water could be heated up to 300° or 400° F., it would produce all the effect of frying. Water, fat, air, and steam are only there as agents to surround the food with required cooking temperatures. Frying conveys heat to upwards of 300°, 400°, and even 500° F. What almost all cooks are doing presently is merely half-frying and half-spoiling the food. If food is immersed in oil which is boiling at 400°, it is sealed with the proofing heat at the moment of contact, allowing no juices to escape and with the heat being transferred simultaneously to every part alike, above and below and on all sides, and providing a crisp unbroken surface *which excludes grease.* Lard is the worst choice of fats for frying even though it does give one of the most characteristic flavors to Mexican food, because it makes the food *look* greasy. Oil is best but it must be heated very slowly and is always apt to boil over. The best of all frying fats is the clarified dripping of roast meat which is as available in some butcher shops as the *pasilla* chile is available in some American groceries. Frying means cooking in hot fat whether it is a nut of butter or a quart of peanut oil. The oil or the fat may be used again and again if it is carefully strained and stored.

FRESA: The strawberry.

FRITO: Fried.

FRIJOL: Bean. There are over sixty kinds of beans to choose from in Mexico. The favorites are: *frijol negro, frijol bayo* (which is approximately a navy bean), and the *frijol canario,* which is like the navy bean as well.

GALLETA: Cracker.

GANSO: Goose.

GARBANZO: Chick-pea.

GARNACHAS: A variety of *antojito.*

GLUCOSA: Corn syrup.

GORDITAS: "Little fatties." A variety of *antojito.*

GRANADILLA: Maypops. The fruit of the passion flower.

GRATINAR: To cover food with cheese, butter, or bread crumbs and brown.

GUACAMOLE: Rhymes with "Ole!" It is the salad one eats with a potato chip, the best part of many soups, the green butter that goes with beef.

GUAJOLOTE: Turkey. The non-Mexican Spanish word is *pavo,* and the breast of either word is immoderately enhanced when smothered in *mole,* the most astonishing turkey gravy ever developed over six thousand years. André Simon says that any large turkey is better stuffed by a taxidermist than by a cook. Turkey with a sausage dressing in England is called an alderman in chains. When the turkey came to France from Mexico it was originally called *poule d'Inde,* which became shortened over the centuries to *dinde* or *dindon.* Even though the turkey was just slightly pagan in origin, being an Aztec bird, it reaches maturity at the end of the year and so became the gastronomic symbol of Christmas.

GUANÁBANA: Soursop. A fruit of the annona family which is outstanding for conserves and ices. There are several popular varieties.

GUAYABA: Guava proves that the best things in life are free: the guava grows wild in Mexico. Guavas are eaten raw but are best candied or taken into the thick fruit pastes called *ates.* They have pink granular meat under yellowish skins, pipped with small seeds.

GUSANO DE MAGUEY: Edible worms from the century plant.

HARINA: Flour or meal.

HELADO: Ice cream.

HIERBAS DE OLOR: One leaf each of oregano, bay, marjoram, and thyme: a *bouquet garni*.

HÍGADO: Liver.

HINOJO: Fennel, a perennial herb of the parsley family. It is not only to be sprinkled over apple pie, bread and rolls, chicken, duck, and fish dishes, but it was believed, in times long gone before, that fennel was an aphrodisiac *and* an enforcer of slenderness. Fennel is also an important vegetable. Its large, bulbous root may be cooked in all the ways of cooking celeriac. Fennel is a delicious vegetable favored with the taste of anise.

HORCHATA: A beverage made with melon seeds, coconut, or whatever fruit is preferred. The fruit, with water, sugar, and lemon, is left to stand for five hours, or as long as overnight, then squeezed through a damp cloth and served with crushed ice.

HONGO: A large mushroom.

HUACHINANGO: Red snapper, easily the most popular fish in Mexico. It reaches perfection as food at the Lincoln Grill in Mexico City, where it is served with a green parsley sauce. Huachinango a la Veracruzana is made with chiles and tomato sauce. It is a fish from the warm Gulf of Mexico which attains a length of three feet at thirty pounds and is frequently served baked whole.

HUEVOS: Eggs have probably nourished more people over the millennia than any other single food. The egg is the symbol of fertility. We eat them, throw them, and smear them on our plows. Eggs are a complete food, easily prepared and digested: a raw egg takes one and a half hours to digest, a baked egg takes five hours. Mexicans are devout about having eggs for breakfast, served with a ranchers' sauce which is a fine combination of tomato puree, tortillas, lard, avocados, *serrano* chiles, onion, garlic, and cheese. That is a sauce to start the day with when you have it with four eggs and some refried beans. The delivery of the first egg as food was one of the major events of civilization. There are 709 ways to prepare an egg for the table. The bravest of these are the Mexican breakfast eggs called *jinetes a caballo con chaparreras* (riders wearing their chaps). The dish contains: 6 toasted tortillas, 12 eggs, 1 pound pork loin, 2 pickled *chipotle* chiles, ½ cup cream, 2 ounces crumbled Jack cheese, a sprig of thyme, ½ pound lard, 3 avocados, 2 *serrano* chiles, 1 tablespoon chopped coriander, 2 tomatoes, 2 onions, 1 large radish, and 1 bay leaf.

IGUANA: A fearsome-looking but gentle lizard about two feet long which makes the most famous stew in the *tierra caliente* regions of Mexico. Iguana tastes like chicken, which, as we know, tastes like veal, which in turn tastes like frogs' legs, which taste like iguana.

JAIBA: Crab, crabmeat. Nature provides: crabs and lobsters come into season as oysters and mussels go out.

Crabs are ready from April to October. The difference between a soft-shell and a hard-shell crab is whether it is caught early or late in the season; the crab sheds its outgrown shell many times as it grows to maturity. Head directly for the Lincoln Grill in Mexico City if you are a crab enthusiast.

JALEA: Aspic and jellies. The name "aspic" means "lavender," not a good seasoning; therefore it was dropped out of aspic making long ago.

JAMÓN: Ham.

JARABE: Syrup.

JENGIBRE: Ginger. The root of the plant is the spice; about ½ hour of cooking is required to release the flavor.

JÍCAMA: A white, sweetish, juicy bulb which is sliced and eaten raw.

JITOMATE: The plump, juicy, normal red tomato of the Colossus of the North.

JOCOQUE: Cottage cheese but with such a much more raffish name.

JUGO: Juice.

JUGO DE NARANJA: Orange Juice.

LAMPREAR: To dress or season with wine.

LANGOSTA: Lobster is a crayfish which might grow to a formidable size, but it lacks claws. Clawed North American lobsters (*Homarus americanus*) get to taste the way they do because they grow in very cold sea water, which the seas around Mexico surely lack. Under the forgetful authors file see Alexandre Dumas, who sometimes wrote so rapidly he could not spare the time to think. He referred to chicken hanging by its "hind legs" and to lobster, which he forgot turns red only when boiled, as "the cardinal of the deep."

LAUREL: Bay leaf. *Laurus nobilis* is the aromatic, sweet bay tree which the Greeks called Daphne, making it a prudent herb because Daphne changed herself into a bay tree to escape the advances of Apollo, a chauvinistic male pig. Bay leaves were the first toupee. Julius Caesar used laurel wreaths to cover his baldness.

LECHE: Milk.

LECHUGA: Lettuce. Should not be eaten in Mexico because it is a vegetable which cannot be peeled of its skin and therefore may not be entirely rid of that sort of fertilizer which causes amebic dysentery.

LENGUA: Tongue.

LENTEJA: Esau's "mess of pottage," the seeds of leguminous plants rich in proteins, vitamin B, iron, and phosphorus.

LEVADURA: Yeast. In Mexico the word is sometimes used to mean baking powder.

LICOR: Liquor.

LIMÓN: Lime. Lemons grow weakly in Mexico but limes are as large as normal lemons and have a more persuasive flavor.

LOMO: Loin, as in loin of pork. However, in Mexico a sirloin is not a *donlomo*.

LONGANIZA: Sausage. Appears in *The Odyssey* of Homer. It seems to have been a black pudding or a *boudin noir* because it is described as being "full of fat and blood." Aristophanes makes an odd plea in his play *The Clouds* when he cries out: "Let them make sausages of me and serve me to the students," which sounds much more as if it should be the speech of that other classical Greek, Spiro Agnew. There are many kinds of sausages, but there is only one *chorizo*, it having been greatly improved over the Spanish version with the addition of chiles. In late Victorian times sausages were called "little bags of mystery" perhaps due to a popular threnody of the period which ran: "Oh, Dunderbeck, oh, Dunderbeck/How could you be so mean/Ever to have invented the sausage meat machine/The water rats and pussycats are no more to be seen/They all were ground to sausage meat in Dunderbeck's machine." Of all sausages, from the Bratwurst to Bologna, the *chorizo* is the gayest, most colorful, and most memorable. It was due to the *chorizo* that one shark groaned to another in the deep sea off Acapulco, "I should never have eaten that last Mexican."

MACHACAR: To crush, to pulverize.

MACERAR: To marinate—and to mash.

MAÍZ: Corn.

MAÍZ DE CACAHUANZINCLE: Hominy.

MAIZENA: Parched corn.

MANDARINA: Tangerine.

MANTECA: Lard.

MANCHA MANTELES: A stew of pork, vegetables, and fruit, freely translated means "stains on the tablecloth."

MANZANA: Apple. Made popular by the trendy young couple Adam and Eve, it is the best known and most useful fruit in the world. The variety called Redstreak was the apple which thunked on Isaac Newton's head, leading to thought in other categories. There are about fourteen hundred varieties of apple. Unlike other fruits, the best apples, and those which keep longest, are those which ripen latest.

MASA: Dough made with corn kernels boiled with lime, then rinsed, skinned, and ground for use as tortillas.

MASCABADO: Unrefined cane sugar.

MECHAR: To wrap meat in bacon or ham.

MEJORANA: Sweet marjoram, the half-sister of oregano. Both are from the mint family, but marjoram is sweeter and more delicate, oregano is lustier and more assertive. Until recently oregano was called wild marjoram.

MELAZA: Molasses.

MELÓN: Cantaloupe or muskmelon.

MEMBRILLO: Quince.

MENEAR: To stir or shake.

MERMELADA: Jam (and marmalade).

MESIOTE: The paper-thin membrane which covers the maguey leaf and is used to wrap meats for barbecuing.

METATE: The flat, slanting stone on which is ground the *nixtamal*, the corn kernels from which the skin has been removed. The corn is ground very fine, then turned into *masa* to become tortillas. Both *nixtamal* and *masa* may be bought by the pound in Mexican stores.

MEZCAL: An intoxicating drink which is made by fermenting then distilling the liquid from the hearts of the maguey plant of the Oaxaca region.

MIEL: Honey, the most natural of sugars, so easily assimilated.

MIGAJÓN: The soft part of bread below the crust.

MIGAJAS: Bread crumbs.

MOLER: To grind.

MOLE: Pronounced mo-lay, the monarch of Mexican sauces, the crown of Mexican food, which, each time it is eaten, is a startling and satisfying experience. It is named from the Aztec word *molli*. There are hundreds of varieties of *mole* in Mexico, many more than there are cheeses in France.

MOLCAJETE: The stone bowl with the ridged interior which is the mortar in which to grind chiles and other food.

MOLINILLO: The beater used to whip chocolate to a froth.

MOSTAZA: Mustard, which, when powdered and dry, has no more savor than cornstarch. Dumas tells that King Louis XI of France took no chances with his hamburgers and always carried a mustard pot with him when he was invited out to dinner, to the grief of his tailor, Sam. The French are the wildest mustard addicts in the world and have developed dozens of different mustard flavors. The mustard eaten by the English is made from a powder developed by Mrs. Clement of Durham in 1729. Mustard, to Mexicans, is something like Devonshire cream to Europeans, a sort of bland confection.

NABO: Turnip.

NARANJA: Orange.

NARANJA CHINA: Kumquat. Even if you don't particularly like them, you must admit that, in either language it is a fruit whose name is a sensual pleasure to speak.

NOPALES: Prickly-pear leaves, which are cooked and eaten as a vegetable.

NUEZ: Walnut.

NUEZ MOSCADA: Nutmeg. Nutmeg and mace come from the same peachlike fruit, *Myristica fragrans*. The nutmeg is enveloped in the mace but weighs much more. Mace has a stronger, more pungent flavor.

ORÉGANO: Sometimes called wild marjoram. Its great popularity today is linked to the pizzas of Naples and American GIs. Oregano grows in wild profusion in Mexico, where some gringos refer to it as Mexican sage. If you are in a practical mood, Pliny prescribed it for scorpion stings. Oregano can be used in all dishes requiring tomatoes. It is among the herbs with considerable clout.

OROZUZ: Licorice.

OSTIONES: Oysters, which, because of unchecked pollution of the seas, are now a lost food. The oyster was a unique being looking like little else as it lay languidly on its left side in oyster beds, without head, ears, eyes, nose, or teeth; yet capable of being polluted that it might poison us. In its day, the oyster created the sort of gastronomic maniac seldom matched. Oysters were opened and gulped as though each one contained a priceless pearl.

PALILLO: Toothpick; see your dentist twice a year.

PALOMA: Dove (the bird, that is, not the past tense of dive).

PAN: Is it a demigod, is it a British paperback book? No, it is bread and, generally, rolls. Mexican rolls are said to have been styled by a European baker imported by the Emperor Maximilian. They are superb. Bread, our great food blessing, gets worse and worse across the Western world, and who else eats it? In many countries (not Ireland) it is necessary to bake one's own bread if what one eats is to resemble good bread. That is, if any of us can remember what good bread was like.

PAPA, PATATA: Potato. Native to Mexico, although the greatest variety of potatoes (in eleven colors) originated in Peru, to be discovered for Europe by the first American gangster, Frankie Pizarro. Today the potato is one of the eight major world food crops. The greatest eaters of potatoes are the people of Ghana, who consumed 2.52 pounds per head per day in 1961–65, the potato having been brought to Ghana by the Portuguese, who got it from the Spanish, who got it you know where.

PAPAYA: A popular Mexican fruit which can weigh ten pounds or more. It is eaten chilled with lemon, is made into a delicious soft drink, and into dulces and conserves. Its commercial use is as a meat tenderizer.

PAPEL: Paper. *Papel encerado* is waxed paper. *Papel de estarza* is brown wrapping paper.

PASA: Raisin.

PASTEL: Cake or pie.

PATO: Duck. Yes, Virginia, Donald Duck is Pato Donaldo in Mexico.

PAVO: Spanish for turkey. Mexican is *guajolote*.

PECHUGA: The breast of fowl. It is also a choice tequila.

PEPINO: Cucumber.

PERA: Pear.

PEREJIL: Parsley, an herb which is not missed until it isn't there. There used to be a hamburger trading post on Fifty-seventh Street in New York which offered this rhyme: "No need to eat your onions sparsely/If you will but chew your parsley." The same place also had a sign about their hamburgers which said, "Served to you in all its delicious goodness on a hot, buttered bum." Parsley inspires rhymes. One, in England, is: "Parsley is garsely." And, "Parsley, parsley, everywhere/Dam, I like my victuals bare." Health-nut food books warn that excessive parsley eating can make one very nervous.

PESCADO: This is fish which has been caught. Not caught, the singular is *pez*, the plural, *peces*. When the Irish died in their potato famine 125 years ago, they had an inexhaustible supply of fine food fish in all the waters around their island which were of little or no use to them. So has it become with the entire planet. By the time we will agree that we will have to be sustained by fish when the population grows to four times its present size, in seventy years' time, the oceans, lakes, and rivers will have been so permanently polluted that the edible fish will have died long since. Australian fish are the prettiest.

PEZ SIERRA: Spanish mackerel.

PICAR: To chop, mince, or hash.

PILONCILLO: Brown, unrefined cane sugar formed into cone-shaped loaves. A syrup made of *piloncillo* and water will replace molasses, and brown sugar moistened with molasses will replace *piloncillo*.

PIMENTÓN: Paprika, one of the capsicum peppers, which originated in Mexico. Paprika is in the chile family, and there are many hundreds in that grouping. Paprika is more of a garnish spice. Its heat factor runs from mild to almost hot and then some when cayenne has been added. Paprika flavors sauces, sour and fresh cream, butter, potatoes, rice, and Hungarians.

PIMIENTA: Black pepper, cayenne, or allspice. Allspice now remains as the only major spice produced exclusively in the western hemisphere. It is the dried, ripe fruit of a very beautiful evergreen tree, the *Pimenta karst,* a myrtle. The dried, hard berry, has a fragrant, pungent taste which is like a mixture of cloves, cinnamon, and nutmeg. It is produced in Mexico and Jamaica. The better allspice is Jamaican.

PIÑA: Pineapple. No one knows with certainty just where in America the pineapple originated. Columbus found it on his second voyage on the island of Guadeloupe, where it was called *ananás.* But the Spanish struck by the fruit's resemblance to pine cones, called it *piña,* which English changed to pine; apple was added to distinguish it from the evergreen tree. The pre-Incans knew the fruit. Pineapples have rich names: the Barbados Sugar Loaf, the Red Spanish, the Bullhead, the Black Antigua, the Puerto Rican Big Head, and the Smooth Cayenne, which is the variety most widely cultivated in Hawaii, where its name was *holokahika,* meaning "screw pine which came from a foreign land." The pineapple is an agavelike plant, which is as Mexican as Tía Carmen's Tuna Pie. When the pineapple decays it develops a virulent, deadly poison which is used by several savage tribes for poisoning arrows and blowgun darts.

PIÑÓN: The pine nut, or Indian nut, which Italians call pinola.

PLÁTANO: Banana, the staple food wherever it grows, is classified as *Musa sapientum,* which means "the fruit of knowledge," which in no way challenges the anecdote about Adam and Eve and the apple because the banana was so named by the ancient Greek philosopher and naturalist Theophrastus, in reporting that the sages of India did all their heavy thinking under the shade of a banana tree. The Koran refers to the banana as "the fruit of Paradise." Bananas were still a novelty in the United States until 1876, when they were exhibited at the Philadelphia Centennial Exposition. Bananas no longer reproduce with seeds but by cultivated grafting.

POLLO: Chicken. Unemployed theologians, incidentally, have solved the riddle "What came first: the chicken or the egg?" It was decided in favor of the egg because all eggs are both innocent and good for food while all chickens are not.

PORO: Leek.

PUERCO: Hog or pig. Very clean, highly intelligent food source which yields his all to feed the world the best proteins and fats. It is legendary that everything but the squeal of the pig is consumed.

PULPA: Flesh. *Pulpa de res* is beef meat.

PULPO: Octopus, cuttlefish.

PULQUE: Fermented juice of the maguey plant, which is mildly intoxicating and useful in some sauces.

QUESO: Cheese, another Mexican product which is best avoided for reasons of undulant fever. The best Mexican cheese is manchego.

QUESADILLA DE FLOR DE CALABAZA: An *antojito* made with yellow squash blossoms.

RÁBANO: Radish. Not much use in Mexican cooking but marvelous eaten raw and for staring at: such a red and such a white against such green leaves.

RALLAR: To grate.

REBOZAR: To coat food in beaten eggs and fry.

RECALENTAR: To reheat. Certain Mexican dishes are required to stand and cool to improve, such as the marvelous *mole* of La Fonda del Refugio in Mexico City—the restaurant, not the humanitarian film star.

RECAUDO: A sauce of onions and tomatoes.

REDUCIR: To cook until excess liquid is evaporated.

RELLENAR: To stuff, as with green peppers. *Antojitos* are usually used to stuff gringos.

REMOLACHA: Red beet. In Spain this is called *betabel* and *betarraga*, but that's their problem.

REMOVER: To stir by rocking or shaking.

REPOLLO: Cabbage, but *col* is more commonly used.

REQUEMAR: To parch or overcook.

RES: Beef.

RIÑONES: Kidneys.

RÓBALO: Haddock.

ROMERITOS: Plants are similar to rosemary but which are eaten as a vegetable.

ROMERO: Rosemary. It is the herb of the women's liberation movement, for the ancient English superstition says: "Where rosemary flourishes, woman rules." How do cultures arrive at maxims like that and make them stick? The delicate temples of the Sleeping Beauty were rubbed with an effusion of rosemary to sober her up and get her back on her feet again. It also goes well with lamb, chicken and seafood.

RUDA: Rue, a seasoning herb.

RUIBARBO: Rhubarb, whose leaves are toxic.

SÁBALO: Shad.

SALCHICHA: Sausage. In Mexico, dachshunds are called *salchichas*.

SALMUERA: Brine.

SALSA: Sauce. Upon his deathbed Brillat-Savarin recast his adage "*A cook can be made but a roaster must be born*" to "*Cooking and roasting are things to teach; it needs genius to make a sauce*," a considerable change of view after a lifetime of reflection. Gravy always means the juices of cooked meats, but a sauce is not always a gravy. The primal sauces from which all others have descended are: brown sauce, called Spanish, and a white one, called velouté. By stretching the fancy one might see it that the great *sauce espagnole* of French cuisine may be one more inspiration from Mexico. When the Bourbons made their way back to the Spanish throne under Louis XV, the French cooks took a hint from the Spanish *olla podrida* and produced a variation of the Spanish brown sauce. Spanish sauces, never particularly abundant, most certainly had been inspired by the greatest brown sauce of gastronomic history, *mole,* just as all Spanish food was influenced by all the other dazzling new variety of food from the Mexican cornucopia. For *mole's* a jolly good *salsa,* that nobody can deny. The Culinary Institute of Mexico City lists 126 other sauces. Sauces may be said to fall into either one of two classifications: (1) the "smother" sauce, and (2) the accompanying, or complementary, sauce. Having survived for well over six thousand years, *mole* is one of the great sauces of all civilizations.

SALTEAR: To sauté. Both the French and Spanish words mean "to leap," as in "Calves' liver leaping in red wine." The word in English would be "to toss," i.e. to fry anything lightly-rapidly in the pan to prevent it from burning, in a sense to cool it from time to to time by tossing, to keep the heat below the temperature of the frying pan.

SAMPSUCO: Marjoram. See oregano.

SANCHOCHAR: To boil in salted water; *cocer* is synonymous.

SANDÍA: Watermelon.

SANGRITA: Tomato and orange juice seasoned with chiles to be used as a chaser for tequila.

SEMILLA: Seed.

SEMOLA: Semolina.

SESOS: Brains.

SOFREÍR: To fry lightly.

SOPA: Soup, and also the starch dish served before the meat course, therefore Mexicans usually refer to the soup as *sopa aquada,* literally "watered soup." Grimod de la Reynière, arch feeder of them all and the Molière of the cookbook, wrote that soup is to dinner what a portico is to a palace, or an overture to an opera; it is only the commencement of the feast but should give an idea of what is to follow. Carême's last words as he plucked at the coverlet were, "Why should the Marquis de Cussy wage war on soup?" The six or seven hundred soups which populate all cookbooks (each time a handful of a different sort of pasta is thrown in, the name of the soup is changed) may be reduced to four basic soups: (1) beef broth or bouillon, (2) double broth or consommé, (3) veal stock, (4) broths made with fowl. The French chemist Parmentier set down this soupmaker's rule: "Let the water be double the meat, a quart for every pound" which is now ordinary practice. Ancient Mexican cuisine offered fruit, squash, and fish soups which were closer to stews.

SOPA DE MÉDULA: Bone marrow soup.

SOPA DE TORTILLA: Similar to *chilaquiles* (which see) or *consommé celestine,* which is made with a garnish of a julienne of pancakes. The tortilla existed long, long before the pancake.

TACO: Emperor of all *antojitos,* the single common denominator of Mexican food because it combines the tortilla and chiles with absolutely everything chewable.

TALLARÍN: Noodle.

TAMALES: Cornmeal containers steamed in corn husks, holding any number of different things, which face the short fate of being wolfed down immediately.

TAMARINDO: Tamarind, an acid, tropic fruit used to flavor soft drinks.

TATAMAR: To cook food in the ground by using a special dish called a *tatemado.*

TEQUEZQUITE: Saltpeter. Potassium nitrate, which is used in cooking vegetables and in puffing doughs for tamales and sponge cakes and is generally used in the Mexican kitchen as a substitute for baking powder.

TEQUILA: Strong booze made by fermenting, distilling, and (it is fervently hoped) redistilling the pulp of the leaf of the century plant.

TERNERA: Veal.

TOCINO: Bacon.

TOMATE VERDE: A small, tart, tomato*like* vegetable which is covered with a dry membrane. It has the effect of counteracting the piquancy of chiles.

TOMILLO: Thyme. The herb of stews and stuffings is one of the triumvirate of the classical *bouquet garni:* three parts parsley to one of thyme and one of bay leaf. The Lady Fair of the **Middle Ages,** she who inspired knights and troubadors, always carried thyme sprigs in her tussie-mussie, held tightly in her hand so that its warmth could release the scent.

TORTA: Mexican sandwich. A long loaf of bread cut in half and filled with chiles, cheese, *frijoles,* meat, *salsa mexicana*—anything and everything.

TORTILLAS: The true "bread" of Mexico, in the form of thin corn pancakes made freshly for each meal and served warm.

TORTUGA: Sea turtle.

TOSTADA: An *antojito* formed by an open-faced toasted tortilla covered with beans, shredded meat, cheese, and so on until ecstasy is defined.

TOTOPOS: Round *antojitos* ranging in size from a silver dollar to a saucer.

TRABAJAR: (Literally, to work.) To beat a sauce until it is smooth.

TRUCHA: Trout.

TUNA: The fruit of the prickly-pear cactus, which grows in different colors. *Tuna cardón* is red. Just under the armor covered with spine is a cool, moist, granular fruit flesh which makes a memorable, not to say immortal, salad, or may be eaten plain.

UNTAR: To oil or butter.

UVAS: Grapes.

UVAS DE CORINTO: Currants, which took their name from the ancient Greek city of Corinth.

UVA ESPINA: Gooseberries.

VAINA: Pod.

VAJILLA: Dinnerware.

VASO: Tumbler.

VENADO: Venison. The misunderstanding that has Sauce Robert being named after a cook goes back to when English and French were freely interchanged because the Normans occupied England, then the English controlled a third of France. Terms were translated beyond recognition. Roebuck sauce, for venison, became Sauce Robert.

VERDOLAGA: Purslane. A potherb which is an essential to Mexican pork dishes.

VERDURAS: Vegetables, either green or leafy.

VINAGRE: Vinegar.

VINO: Wine. If you go to Mexico, try to drink chilled San Marcos *Violeta,* a dry amethyst rosé which is grown in Aguascalientes' crazy "hot" soil. It is light and quite the best of all Mexican wines.

XOCONOXTLE: A sour *tuna* used in *moles.*

ZANAHORIAS: Carrots.

I move the telescope
to the waxing crescent moon:
a perfect sliver of possibility.

                        "It's clear," I say to Harriet.
                        "You should come and see."

But Harriet lies
on her back,
dangling her legs
over the edge,
making the canopy rustle
in the night breeze.

"I'm busy," she sighs,
her eyes on her phone,

                        missing the stars
                            shining bright
                            right above us.